SCHOOL BUILDERS

SCHOOL BUILDERS

ELEANOR CURTIS

Ⓦ WILEY-ACADEMY

Acknowledgements

Thanks to Jan Scharf and especially to Famida Rasheed for assistance in the research of schools; Clifford Pearson of *Architectural Review*, US, for some very useful suggestions; and to Annette Brauenig for assistance with the German texts.

Thanks to all the architects and their helpers for organising the material and responding to my requests; especially to Ray C Bordwell and Ralph Johnson of Perkins & Will's Chicago office, and Steve Clow and Nev Churcher of Hampshire County Council Architects. And finally thanks to my editor Maggie Toy for her patience, and all at John Wiley who have suggested projects and assisted with editorial and production.

Illustration Credits

Every effort has been made to locate sources and credit material but in any cases where this has not been possible our apologies are extended. All drawings are courtesy of the first-named architects or engineers, as are all the photographs except the following: Cover: © Martine Hamilton-Knight; Frontispiece: © Hedrich Blessing; p. 6 Christian Kandzia, courtesy of Behnisch & Partners; p. 8, © Chew I Jin; p. 10 top left, Tomio Ohashi, courtesy of Itsuko Hasegawa Atelier; p. 10 top centre, Ethan Kaplan © SMWM; p. 11 bottom centre, Christian Kandzia, courtesy of Behnisch & Partners; p. 11 bottom right, © James Dow; p. 12 top, Timothy Hursley and Richard Barnes, © SMWM; p. 12 bottom, © Milroy-McAleer; p.14 bottom left and bottom right, courtesy of plus+ bauplanung; p. 18 bottom, © Caroline Sohie/Roland Reinardy, courtesy of Arup Associates; p. 20 bottom, © Michael Krüger; p. 22 bottom, Rainer Mader, © Thomas van den Valentyn; pp. 26-27, © Nev Churcher; p. 30, © Tim Soar; p. 38, Espen Tharaldsen; p. 39, Jim Bengston; p. 39, Espen Tharaldsen; pp. 41-43, Jim Bengston; p. 44, Jiri Havran; pp. 45-46 Jim Bengston; p. 47, Jiri Havran; pp.48-49, 51-53, Jonathan Moore, courtesy of Architecture PLB; pp. 54-57, © Caroline Sohie/Roland Reinardy courtesy of Arup Associates; pp. 58-60, pp. 62-77, Christian Kandzia, courtesy of Behnisch & Partners; pp. 78-87, © Martine Hamilton-Knight; pp. 88-90, 92-95, © Milroy-McAleer; pp. 96, 98-102, © David Churchill and Keith Hunter; pp. 103-106, 108-118, © Nev Churcher; pp. 119-124, © Hein Goldstein Architekt; pp. 125-127, Tamatau Kurumada, courtesy of Itsuko Hasegawa Atelier; pp. 128, Albert Lim; pp. 130-133, © Chew I Jin; pp. 135-139, © Jonathan Hillyer/Esto; pp. 140-143, 145-147, © James Dow; pp. 148-155, © Hedrich Blessing; pp. 156-157, 159-163, 165, © Hedrich Blessing; pp. 166-167, 169-173, © Hedrich Blessing; pp. 174-189, courtesy of plus+ bauplanung; pp. 190-195, Steve Hall, Hedrich Blessing, © Hedrich Blessing, Steve Hall; pp. 196-202, Steve Hall, Hedrich Blessing, © Hedrich Blessing, Steve Hall; pp. 202-204, Ethan Kaplan, © SMWM; pp. 205-206, Timothy Hursley and Richard Barnes, © SMWM; pp. 207-213, Rainier Mader, © Thomas van den Valentyn; pp. 214-221, © Michael Krüger.

Cover: Hampden Gurney School, London, England, Building Design Partnership
Frontispiece: Perry Community Education Village, Perry, Ohio, US, Perkins & Will

Other Wiley Editorial Offices

John Wiley & Sons Inc., 111 River Street, Hoboken, NJ 07030, USA

Jossey-Bass, 989 Market Street, San Francisco, CA 94103-1741, USA

Wiley-VCH Verlag GmbH, Boschstr. 12, D-69469 Weinheim, Germany

John Wiley & Sons Australia Ltd, 33 Park Road, Milton, Queensland 4064, Australia

John Wiley & Sons (Asia) Pte Ltd, 2 Clementi Loop #02-01, Jin Xing Distripark, Singapore 129809

John Wiley & Sons Canada Ltd, 22 Worcester Road, Etobicoke, Ontario, Canada M9W 1L1

Design and Prepress: ARTMEDIAPRESS Ltd, London

Printed and bound in Italy

CONTENTS

PREFACE

This volume is about school buildings and school builders over the last fifteen years of design and construction, and the design issues facing school builders of today.

The projects presented here were selected on their ability to demonstrate explicitly one or another issue relevant to contemporary school design, and on the architects' availability to participate in the gathering of information necessary for inclusion. There are many more school projects out there that I would have liked to have included but have had neither space nor time to do so. In addition, there are many more countries and educational philosophies I would have liked to have covered but have been unable to within this volume.

However, I would like to think that the wide range of school projects gathered together here in one volume will give architects, school commissioners, head teachers and even parents an idea of the wonderful design solutions possible in response to the typically disciplined brief for school buildings.

It should be noted that information pertaining to 'Project Information' is as accurate and informed as possible, and that not all project facts are complete. The cost of each project has been left in its own currency rather than converted into one single currency. In addition, some project descriptions have been provided by the architects themselves, but are not explicitly credited.

Vocational School, Öhringen, Germany, Behnisch & Partner

Lycée Français de Singapour

INTRODUCTION

At the beginning of the 1990s, C William Brubaker, late principal architect of US firm Perkins & Will and an expert in school design, listed the significant changes in school programmes and policies that influenced approaches to school design between the 1960s and the 1990s (*School and College*, May 1992). These sum up the many generic issues relevant to the building and designing of schools, and are particularly useful in providing a basis from which to compare. The list is summarised as follows:

Curriculum-driven changes

Then...

Teaching was based on books and standard classrooms.

Now...

Teaching and learning methods are changing school design. With the advent of the use of new technologies in schooling (especially the computer) there are new demands for flexibility of space.

Specialised spaces

Then...

There were many standard classrooms.

Now...

There are more specialised spaces tailored to different subjects, for example art, technology and science.

Special education

Then...

Special education schools or spaces were built for special needs students.

Now...

Special needs students are taught within standard classrooms and laboratories.

Variety

Then...

School buildings conformed mostly to 'barrack-style' or rectangular block plans.

Now...

There is more variety and choice of school buildings, including special types of schools, for example vocational high schools, music schools, Montessori schools and church schools.

Class size

Then...

Large, overcrowded schools often had class sizes of 30 and more.

Now...

Teachers and parents have demanded reduced class sizes.

School size

Then...

Schools were getting larger with extensions to existing schools.

Now...

Size has been re-evaluated. Small schools have a more 'human' scale and are more flexible.

Regulations

Then...

School buildings were less regulated.

Now...

Design for new school buildings is more complex due to many new regulations, for example access for people with disabilities, fire safety, building codes, energy use, air quality, coastal zone regulations, environmental impact and area requirements.

Costs

Then...

Student-per-year costs were high due to increasing operational and maintenance costs.

Now...

Student-per-year costs are lower due to reduced operational and maintenance costs.

The all-year school

Then...

Schools were used only for the nine-month school year.

Now...

Schools may be open for 12 months a year and used by the local community during non-academic months.

Electronic links

Then...

Schools stood alone.

Now...

Schools may be electronically linked to other schools, administrative offices, libraries, colleges and universities, and other cities and countries, for example via the Internet.

Energy efficiency

Then...

School buildings were thin-walled, poorly insulated energy hogs.

Now...

New school buildings tend to be 'green' in their approach and well insulated, well ventilated and energy efficient.

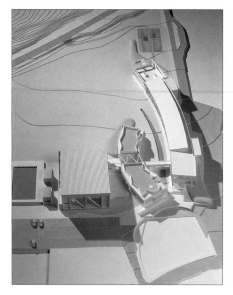

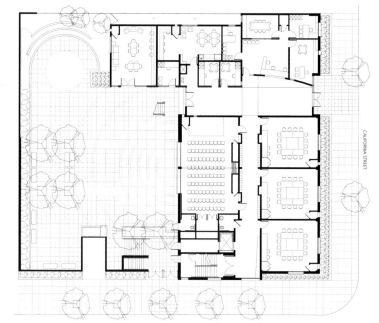
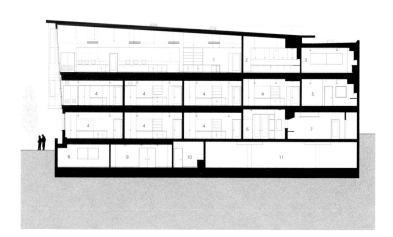

Top left Kaiho Elementary School

Top centre, right and bottom Drew College Preparatory School

Ten years have passed since Brubaker's list, and the changes he outlined have continued to evolve. In fact, it would be fair to say that educational policies and trends in education are continually changing, and in turn affecting the design of schools.

However, it is the use of new technologies in education that has been, and continues to be, the main driving force behind the more extreme and rapid changes of recent years. Technology has allowed schools and learning to change, in the sense of both physical space and the type of activity taking place in that space. Learning can now happen in many different spaces, using many different tools, and at different times for groups or for individuals. In addition, the hardware and software for the tools are constantly changing, making new demands on the space.

Beyond the demands of technology, there are many other contemporary issues to be accommodated: for example the relationship of the local community to the school, now vital for its success; the fashion and political correctness of adopting a 'sustainable' approach; the challenge of creating safe and healthy schools in dense urban environments; and an ever-increasing number of students to accommodate.

The most common challenge to school builders of today, a challenge that encompasses all of the above factors is the demand for 'flexibility' in the design of the school. Schools need to be able to accommodate potential changes in technology, demographics, green policies, urban regeneration, safety and security, and all within (mostly) public budgets. And on top of this, they need to do so using creative design solutions.

The schools presented in this volume begin to deal with most of these issues, and as a result a number of them are quite outstanding.

FLEXIBILITY

The term 'flexibility' is these days often used by architects to describe the design of their buildings, but its meaning is seldom clarified. However, when dealing with the ever-changing demands of today's learning environments it would be useful to understand both what is really meant by 'flexibility' and whether a school can be truly flexible in design as a response to need.

Consider the flexibility demanded by other public spaces, for example the office space, which is marketed to a range of different clients on the basis that it may be adapted according to need. The space must be able to adapt to technological changes (wiring, cabling, networks and communications), to a variety of plumbing and electrical needs, be well insulated and adequately ventilated, and perhaps be extended or reduced in floor area according to need.

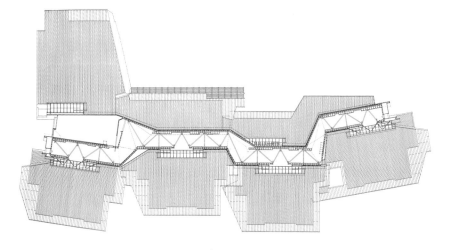

Top and bottom right Strawberry Vale
Elementary School

Bottom left and centre Montessori
School Ingolstadt

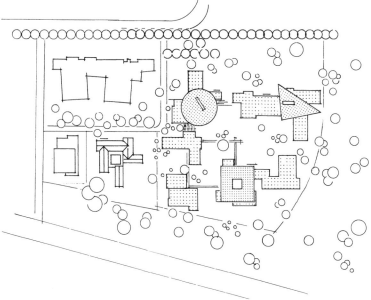

Similarly, changes in school curricula demand different things from the built environment, and like the real market some of these are not foreseeable.

It is the job of architects to accept and work with the challenge that what they build today in the (continually changing) education sector must be able to adapt easily to the needs of tomorrow. They can do this only if they have an intelligent and thorough understanding of what is required of the physical environment in order for teachers to educate and students to learn.

Some clear examples in which the classroom space is designed to be flexible include Itsuko Hasegawa's designs for Kaiho Elementary School, where the classrooms have moveable partitions so that the space may be expanded or contracted according to need, and architects SMWM's response to the limited site area in its design of flexible seating arrangements for Drew College Preparatory School in San Francisco.

In the case of the more remote setting of Strawberry Vale by Patkau Architects, the elementary school is designed to allow mobile carts in and out of spaces, and these are 'plugged in' to classrooms or common areas for the teaching of specialised subjects.

Where there is limited space or more than one learning tool, classrooms may need to accommodate more than one activity at the same time. The L-shaped classroom is one solution to this, the second activity taking place around the corner of the 'L'. Indeed, US firm Perkins & Will's first school project (Crow Island School in Winnetka, Illinois, US), built in 1938, used L-shaped classrooms to house large built-in storage units within the classroom.

Interestingly, none of the projects featured in this volume have adopted this particular design, but have used other flexible forms including wet and dry areas (Woodlea Primary School), inside and outside decks (Woodlea Primary School, Whiteley Primary School, Stakes Hill Infant School, Montessori School Ingolstadt and Strawberry Vale Elementary School), and the moveable partitions of Kaiho Elementary School.

TECHNOLOGY

As mentioned above, the need for flexibility in the design of schools is predominantly the result of the introduction of new technologies and new telecommunications tools – the ever-changing tools for education.

Rapid advances in software and hardware affect the way in which a child can learn psychologically as well as the physical spaces required. Indeed, the use of new technologies in education allows a broader range of subject options while, in relative terms, demanding less physical space.

Introduction

And students may now have tutorials direct from the computer, learning on an individual basis at their own pace.

New schools today usually dedicate a room or centre for computer use and/or video or other media equipment. And the majority of middle schools presented in this volume include the more recent addition of a 'media centre' to the campus (see below). Alternatively, some school classrooms have computer links and video facilities in every classroom (see Rio del Norte Elementary School by Dougherty & Dougherty Architects LLP).

On top of all this, the library has 'got wise'. The library is no longer seen as a remote part of the school to be visited now and then for homework, but is rather an extension to the classroom, offering other means for learning and learning by doing. Its contents can now be researched via the computer, which requires computer desk terminals, and generally there are more individual study spaces for students.

With the advent of online books, libraries no longer need the same 'stack space' that they once did, and as the size of the library decreases the space for alternative media rooms increases. In response to this, some schools have dedicated an entire block or cluster for the 'media centre' – an umbrella term for the library, computer facilities, audio-visual facilities, art and music rooms (see Perkins & Will and Goldstein). Regarding design issues, some school architects have favoured a bookshop-style or cyber-café-type library, giving the space more colour and character than it might otherwise be able to offer (see SMWM Architects).

SIZE

Does the size of a school really matter? Popular opinion in the 1960s supported the idea of 'the bigger the better' school because it was assumed that the larger the school, the greater the choice of subjects and extra curricular activities it would be able to offer. However, attitudes to size have changed substantially in recent years, perhaps mainly due to the use of new technologies that allow a broader range of subject options for students without demanding as much space – schools can now achieve more in less space.

So what is the ideal number of students for a school campus? There are many arguments in favour of the smaller school, for example it is claimed that the greatest number of discipline problems occur when students change classes and travel from one part of the school to the other, problems which can be reduced in smaller schools where students can travel shorter distances to fewer classrooms, or may even remain in the same classroom for all subjects. In addition, the smaller the school the easier it is for the students to identify with it, and the easier it is to control their behaviour. Sustainability issues are also more manageable in a smaller school.

But not all school commissions are for small schools, so what is the best approach when the brief is for a large school? Does this necessitate a large campus with rows of classrooms, long corridors and repetitive blocks of buildings? Or can it yield creative design solutions?

SPLIT SITE

A very interesting design solution by architects Perkins & Will for the 1,800 pupils of Desert View Elementary School in New Mexico was to split the school into many sites. Three identical facilities were repeated about a quarter of a mile apart from each other, utilising readily available land parcels. This idea was feasible given the availability and economics

Top Lick-Wilmerding High School

Bottom Rio del Norte Elementary School

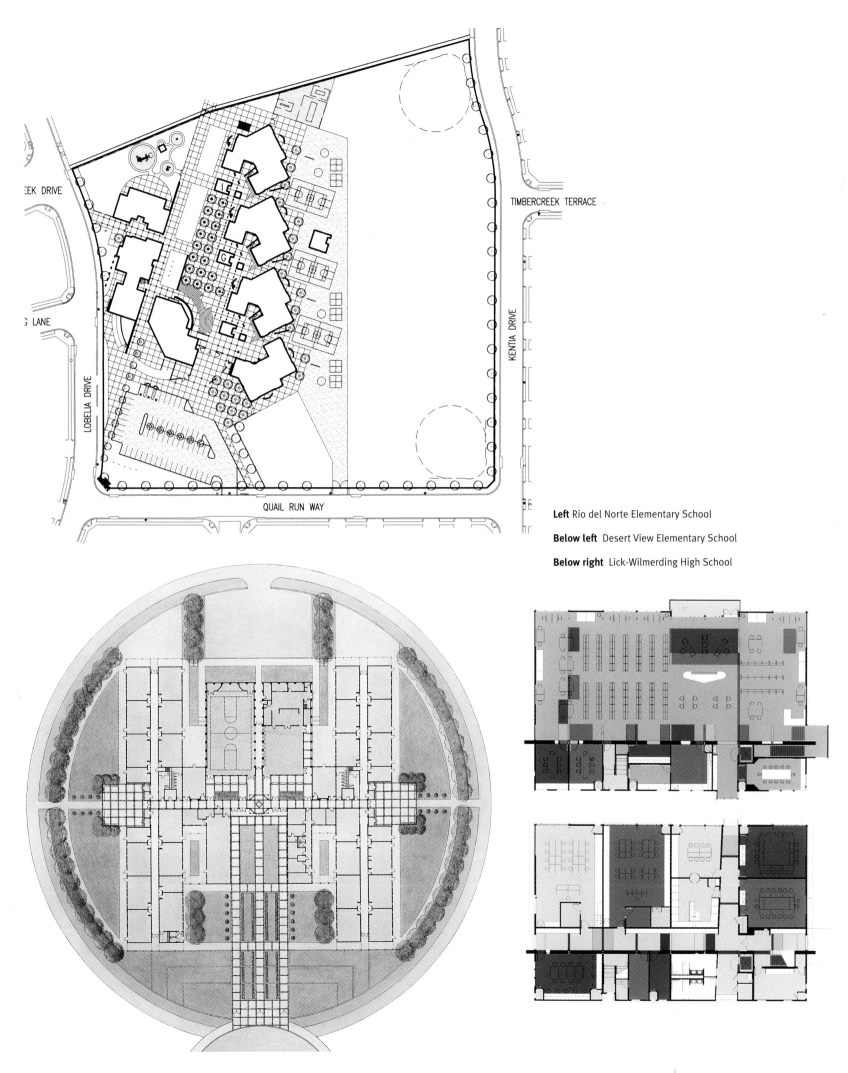

Left Rio del Norte Elementary School

Below left Desert View Elementary School

Below right Lick-Wilmerding High School

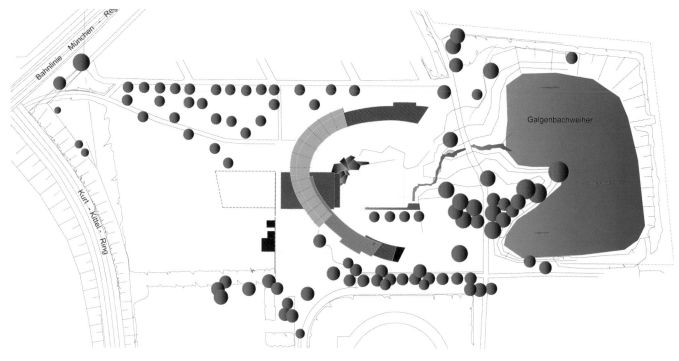

Top Oskar-Maria-Graf-Gymnasium

Centre and bottom right Evangelische Gesamtschule Gelsenkirchen

Bottom left Waldorf School

School Builders

Top Lycée Français Singapour

Bottom Haute Vallée School

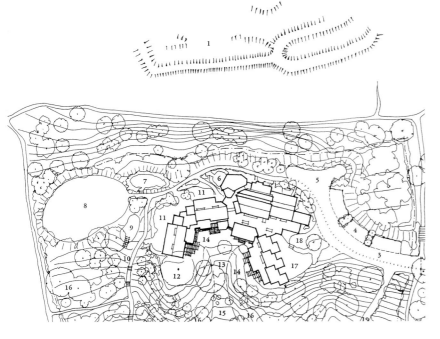

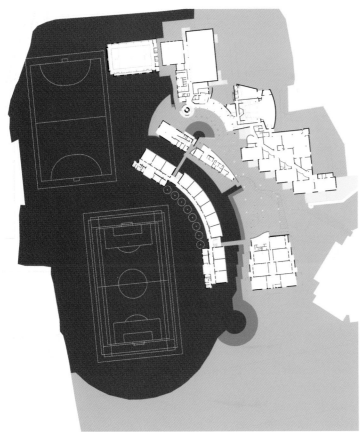

of acquiring local land, and because the student population was an accumulating figure so that not all three schools had to be ready at exactly the same time.

ALL IN ONE

Many schools are large because they cater for students from kindergarten age through elementary and high school on one campus. Here, there might be obvious site and architectural divisions between the three schools but with shared facilities. The Lycée Français (International French School) in Singapore by Kumpulan Akitek gives distinct architectural form to each school with the aim that the students will be able to identify with their own school.

This idea of one large campus for many schools can also reduce maintenance costs as power output from a centralised plant can be shared, and is a way for handling huge student numbers. Perkins & Will's design for the 4,500 students of the lower, middle and high schools for Perry Community Education Village in Ohio, as its name suggests was conceived as an 'education village' rather than as a single school. Here, as with the Lycée Français Singapour (International French School of Singapore), the three schools are differentiated by way of plan but in contrast to the Singapore school, recognisable building types have been used throughout each to create a unified identity.

A MINIATURE VILLAGE

Another popular design solution for the large campus is to model the school on a small village, with clusters of buildings and a central 'street' or pedestrian spine. Organising classrooms and other facilities in clusters may also reduce the distance a student has to travel for class changeovers, limiting the opportunities for students to become distracted. Concentrating activities in one part of a large campus may also encourage students to feel a sense of belonging to the school and a greater sense of identity.

Designs by plus+ bauplanung for the 1,300-student Evangelische Gesamtschule Gelsenkirchen (Evangelical School in Gelsenkirchen) use the idea of the school as a village, with school buildings clustered around a central covered piazza. Rooms and workshops are conceived as though shops on a street. The firm's second school in this volume, the Waldorf School in Cologne for 450 students, uses the idea of the central spine running between some of the main buildings. The plan concentrates on a central, skylit hall, which is also the main meeting space for students and is similar to the central piazza idea.

In contrast, instead of using the regular forms of streets and shops, Architecture PLB's site plan for the 750-student Haute Vallée School in Jersey is a series of curves and geometric shapes dissected by the central spine, the end result having more in common with a cluttered urban centre.

For the design of their North Fort Myers School, Florida, which can take 1,600 students, Perkins & Will had to take into account the existing school buildings. To manage the size of the campus, buildings were organised around a new media centre, which became the 'heart' of the school. Similarly, in Hein Goldstein's design for the 900-student Oskar-Maria-Graf-Gymnasium (Oskar-Maria-Graf Secondary School) in Neufahrn, Germany, the centrepiece is the art centre sited in the central courtyard with the school looking in.

Lord, Aeck & Sargent take the idea of the miniature village to the extreme in their 500-student Trinity School in Atlanta. Faced with a challenging and difficult site, the new additions to this elementary school adopted a fairytale-type typography giving the school a very distinct identity with castle-like walls and towers. Rather than a small village, part of it looks like a small gothic castle!

URBAN REGENERATION

The commissioning of new schools can be part of urban regeneration programmes, especially in low-income areas. Here, expectations of the final design are much higher in terms of connecting with the local community and restoring/defining a new identity for the area. In addition, schools with a high proportion of pupils from low-income families are often expected to provide services beyond formal education: schools in areas with sizeable populations of immigrants may need to provide language support for non-native-speaking pupils, to provide primary healthcare and a safe environment.

Working in inner-city crime-ridden neighbourhoods, Ross Barney + Jankowski Inc have used some very simple design ideas to bring the school closer to the local community. For example, the playground of Cesar Chavez Elementary School in Chicago was placed in front of the school building and not behind or enclosed by it, as is often the case, so that the children were in full view of both classrooms and nearby homes. Bright colours were used for the exterior and interior, which complemented the local Mexican culture and gave the school an extra sense of significance for the children.

Ross Barney + Jankowski's second project in this volume is also set in the heart of Chicago's Mexican community. With a limited site area, the architects have literally 'reached out' to the local community by bringing the school building right to the edge of the pavement. The theme is a play on the sun, which is common to Mexican culture. Again, bright colours are used mostly in the grand stairwell but also on the sunburst terrazzo floor.

VERTICAL SOLUTIONS

Limited site area is a common problem for architects building in the city. Ross Barney + Jankowski have dealt with this by bringing the school to the edge of the pavement (see above), and in a separate project by building another, higher storey resulting in a greater proportion of exterior wall than most school buildings yet achieving the same square footage.

Other architects have gone vertical in their designs. Hampden Gurney School in central London (Building Design Partnership) replaced a one- and two-storey building with a six-storey school, each level affording outdoor, safe and weather-proof play-deck terraces adjacent to the classrooms, with a further play deck on the roof. Similarly, Elder and Cannon Architects designed St Aloysius Junior School in central Glasgow to be light and airy, despite its inner-city location. The five-storey school is organised vertically and uses a triple-height stairwell to afford light to the interior. The five-storey south elevation maximises the infusion of air and light into the classes but is also layered to give shade and privacy.

With only a small site to work with, SMWM made the best of what little space was available in their design for the new Drew College Preparatory School. A three-storey L-shaped structure with a courtyard, the classrooms ended up small, but have flexible seating arrangements to compensate. The architects have also maximised the advantages of having a corner axis, and have built a double-height, light-filled library.

IMPOSING SITES

Schools can be situated in undesirable locations, particularly in areas where land is both precious and pricey. When space is tight but there is a need for a substantial school, land parcels will be found on the outskirts of the town, typically where the town meets industry or highways.

The Vocational School in Öhringen (Behnisch & Partner) is located on the outskirts of a town, with an elevated highway, a shopping centre, several industrial buildings and a few residences nearby. The architects have tried to counteract the unattractive mix of the surrounding built environment by giving the school a strong identity of built form: the building curves away from the highway and embraces an interior court, the surrounding inner curve of which is light and colourful.

This sweeping plan has also been used by Hein Goldstein as a design solution to the ugly surrounds of his Oskar-Maria-Graf-Gymnasium in Neufahrn. The site, also on the edge of town, suffers noise from three sides in the form of a railway line, a ring road and a sports ground. In response, the school curves away from the noise and embraces a small lake on the other side.

In an extreme example, Perkins & Will were faced with a nuclear power plant as the nearest neighbour to the Perry Community Education Village in Ohio. Instead of completely rejecting this industrial form, which is visible from the school grounds, a slim tower marks the entrance to school's theatre and sports centre as a counterpoint to the cooling towers of the nuclear plant across the landscape. (In fact, the school was funded by the revenues generated by the nuclear plant.)

AFTER-HOURS AND COMMUNITY INVOLVEMENT

Traditionally, schools tended to be locked up at the end of the school day, in the middle or late afternoon. However, it is logical that the local community be allowed to make use of the facilities schools offer for continuing education or recreation clubs (theatre groups, music and sports clubs).

Opening facilities after-hours can also bring the local community closer to the school, and this is especially relevant in low-income urban environments where the school has been typically placed away from the urban neighbourhood due to restricted availability of a suitable site 'downtown'. Where a school is located downtown, sharing its facilities makes much more economical sense for both school and community.

Building the relationship between the school and the local community is critical for staff and students alike, and getting this right means involving the community in the early stages of design. For example, Allford Hall Monaghan Morris's brief for the Great Notley Primary School in Essex required the involvement of the end-users of the school right from the start. However, this proved difficult; as the school was new, the school community did not yet exist. To solve this, the architects used a mock-user group of teachers and heads from other schools.

The Evangelische Gesamtschule Gelsenkirchen by plus+ bauplanung demonstrates the most direct involvement of students in the design process. The architects' proposals were based on the ideas of the children, and from these the children then built-up models. The designs were then adjusted by the architects in accordance with building regulations before the building contractors began construction. All interior finishings were decided by teachers, parents and students. The same firm's Waldorf School in Cologne also involved teachers, parents and children in the design process, and the tiled floor of Woodlea Primary School, by Hampshire County Council Architects, included children's designs executed by an invited artist.

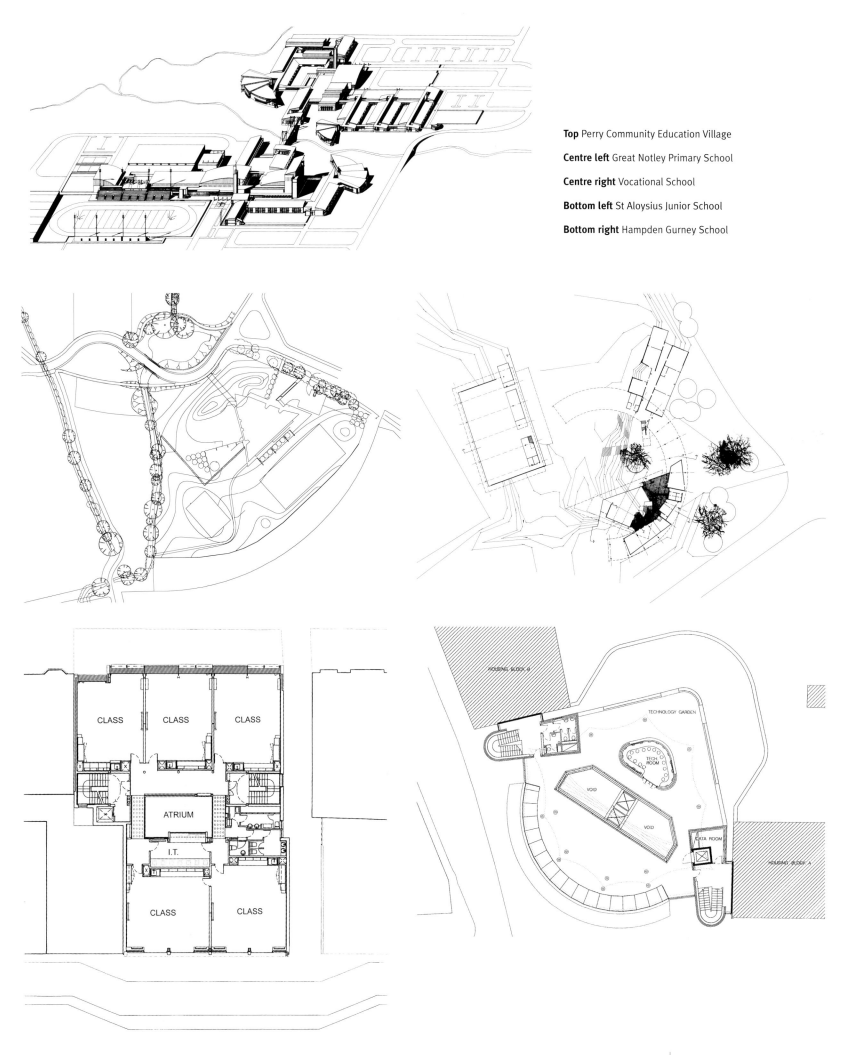

Top Perry Community Education Village

Centre left Great Notley Primary School

Centre right Vocational School

Bottom left St Aloysius Junior School

Bottom right Hampden Gurney School

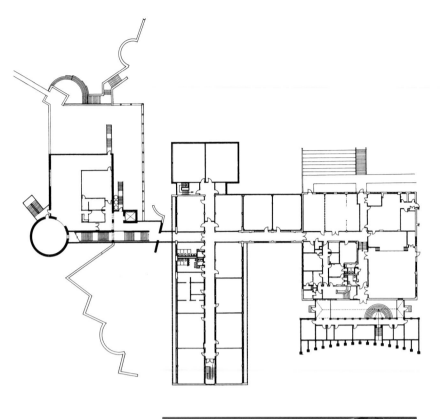

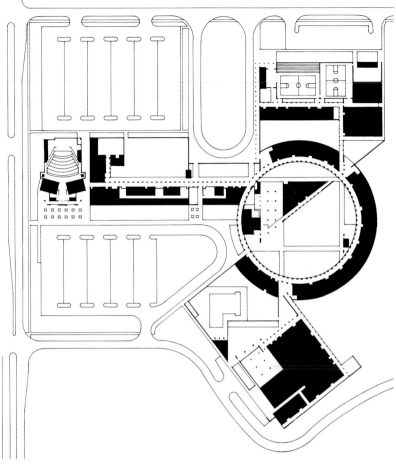

Top left Trinity School

Top right North Fort Myers School

Bottom Druk White Lotus School

LEARNING THROUGH LANDSCAPE

School buildings are more than just a built form for education – they are total learning environments that use a variety of gadgets and settings as the source of learning. Learning is not confined to the classroom: it can take place within the great halls, in the corridors, the cafeterias, the gymnasiums, the library and the natural landscape.

Learning through landscape is wonderfully expressed in many schools presented in this volume, often promoting outdoor learning and encouraging students to be involved with the development of the landscape, as part of the overall design of the school.

Itsuko Hasegawa talks about 'architecture as topography' in her designs for Kaiho Elementary School in Himi, Japan. She sees her architecture as part of an overall landscape design, rather than the landscape design following on from the architecture, and hopes that students will use this 'garden school' to its full potential.

Nev Churcher of Hampshire County Council Architects, responsible for Woodlea Primary School, talks about 'giving in' to the surrounding landscape and working within nature's given boundaries. The results of his approach can be seen in the wonderful shapes and forms of the school, which fit beautifully into the surrounding woods. All classrooms have

external covered 'decks' allowing children and teachers to work outdoors. (Stakes Hill Infant School, also by Hampshire County Council Architects, also uses outdoor decks.)

Behnisch & Partner's Montessori School in Ingolstadt uses the outdoor deck idea for its 'green' classrooms, which are further protected by hedges and tall shrubs. Each classroom has its own special tree, which gives it an individual identity and also affords some shade.

Children have also been involved in the development of the gardens of the Evangelische Gesamtschule in Gelsenkirchen (plus+ bauplanung). Here the schoolchildren are required to grow vegetable, herb or flower gardens as part of their education. Similarly, the environmental studies programme offered by North Fort Myers School, designed by Perkins & Will, has accommodated the architects' landscape design of the 'experimental garden' and preserved wetlands on-site.

SLOPING SITES

The landscape can be used and exploited in the overall design of the school, adding another dimension to this field of architecture; for example, where there are sloping sites, school buildings must accommodate these in some form or another.

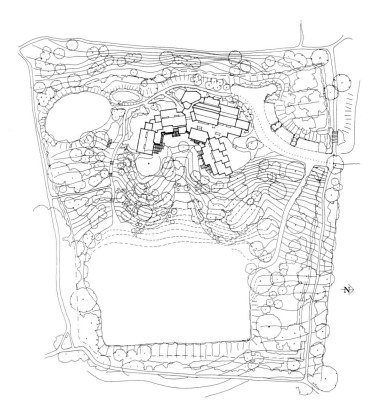

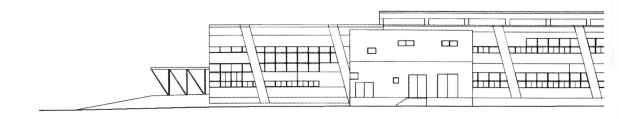

Top left Woodlea Primary School

Top right Whiteley Primary School

Bottom Stakes Hill Infant School

At Woodlea Primary School, Hampshire County Council Architects have worked with a sharp slope and a natural 'bowl', and have cleverly adapted the design around these features. The building follows the contours of the natural bowl using ramped circulation to connect spaces, and distinctly changes levels (just a metre apart) only twice. Stakes Hill Infant School, also by Hampshire County Council Architects, accommodates a steep slope. The building design follows the slope with its timber buildings increasing above ground level as the site slopes away. It has exploited the upper end of one building wing by providing storage units for outdoor sports equipment. Strawberry Vale Elementary School in British Columbia (Patkau Architects) is located on a more gentle slope, which is also incorporated into the design with the use of ramps.

However, more challenging than a gentle slope was the gorge Lord, Aeck & Sargent were faced with when designing new buildings for Trinity School in Atlanta, Georgia. Taking the gorge as the source for inspiration, rather than being overwhelmed by its imposition, the gymnasium and media centre/library hugs the 12-metre (40-foot) drop of the gorge on the inside and presents a decorative immense wall on the outside. Traversed with bridges and with outdoor stairs spiralling down the tower to its floor, the gorge has become a key feature and has made the new buildings fun and interesting.

GREEN SCHOOLS AND SUSTAINABILITY

Other fashionable terms used in architecture today are 'sustainability' and 'green' design. A very broad and basic definition of these terms might include energy efficiency, resource efficiency, health, and educating children and staff with regard to green practices, which must be present and visible at the start of the design and build cycle, and not simply in the end result. (At Whiteley Primary School, by Hampshire County Council Architects, the design, use and development of the whole school environment were in fact used for teaching about sustainability.)

Perhaps the most striking example of design sustainability is the Druk White Lotus School in Ladakh, India, by Arup Associates (London). This is an unusual and praiseworthy project located beneath the western Himalayas of northern India. Being so remote, the school's entire infrastructure had to be created from scratch keeping in mind the fact that it needed to be sustainable within such an environment. Arup have used their technology-based high-level analysis to solve some of the problems of the project using traditional materials, for example, analysis of the seismic performance of materials, solar energy, passive heating and cooling and water recycling. Local stone and mud bricks have been used as construction materials, and the cost of the school is estimated to be one-tenth of what it would cost to build in Europe.

Sustainability of design has been high on the agenda in various projects by Hampshire County Council Architects, Allford Hall Monaghan Morris, Patkau Architects, Architecture PLB, plus+ bauplanung and Arbeidsgruppen HUS. Common throughout all these projects is the careful siting, layout and sections of the buildings in order to take into consideration the microclimate and passive solar management. Other design issues include ensuring good insulation in floors, walls and roofs to reduce energy consumption, and using sustainable and durable materials.

The use of local and natural materials is an especially visible example of a green approach. However, as Nev Churcher, architect of both Woodlea and Whiteley Primary Schools by Hampshire County Council Architects, points out, natural materials are not always the most hard wearing or sustainable. Sometimes synthetic materials are greener than natural ones, in that they have a much longer life than their natural counterparts (see 'Talks with:', p 26).

Allford Hall Monaghan Morris, the architects of Great Notley Primary School in Essex, came across the unexpected problem that natural materials robust enough for the design cannot always be found locally, and therefore acquiring them can be more costly in terms of the energy used to import them. In contrast to this, Patkau Architects were fortunate enough to have easy access to wood – the most readily accessible and renewable construction material available in British Columbia, Canada – for its Strawberry Vale Elementary School, which is a wonderful example of the use of natural materials.

The architects at Norway's Arbeidsgruppen HUS, working in a very cold northern climate, have tried very hard to create 'breathable' walls that allow for the better circulation of air for both students and for the materials used, and have therefore designed walls with many layers, each layer with its own function, to encourage the circulation of air.

But sustainability must also relate to the flexible nature of a school's design: architects must consider whether potential changes to the classroom configurations will be difficult to achieve or costly. Changes to the design should be welcomed and not discouraged. Building materials and furniture should be selected on the basis that they may be used for many different activities, either now or in the future.

SAFETY AND SECURITY

Security has become an important issue in the design of the schools of today. The traditional 'openness' of schools has been lost as a result of tragic disasters, yet architects need to strike a balance. How do they balance the need for a sense of freedom and/or freewill for the students versus the need for tight security?

Ralph Johnson of Perkins & Will has demonstrated one solution to this in his design of North Fort Myers School in Florida. Though its courtyards are locked at night, the school is essentially open in its design, using a vocabulary of covered walkways, breezeways and slender columns. Dougherty & Dougherty eliminated the need for a protective fence for the Rio del Norte Elementary School by configuring the site around an inner courtyard; although it is not always ideal to have the school facing inwards in a complete sense, this is necessary in some cases. And Zvi Hecker's designs for the Jewish Primary School in Berlin have created a very safe and secure environment by using the very 'open' and creative metaphor of the flower, the folds of which orient inwards and away from the world. The majority of the schools featured in this volume have taken into consideration such security issues, more relevant today for schools than perhaps ever before. The main difference between schools of yesterday and

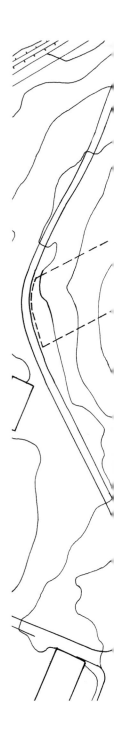

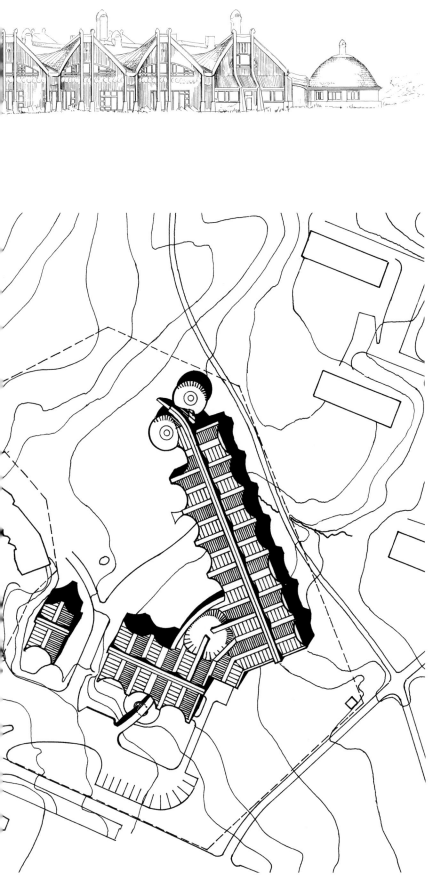

Above Jewish Primary School

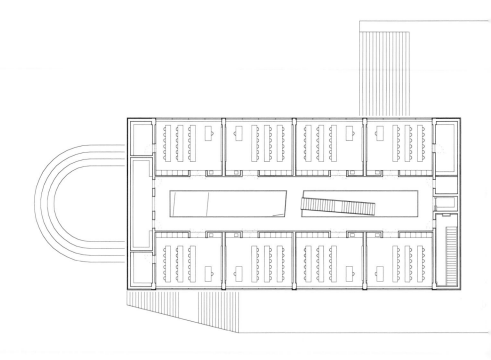

Musikgymnasiums Schloß
Belvedere bei Weimar

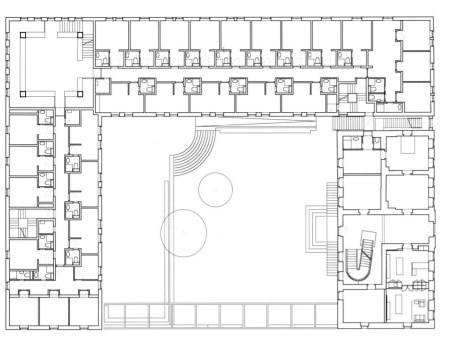

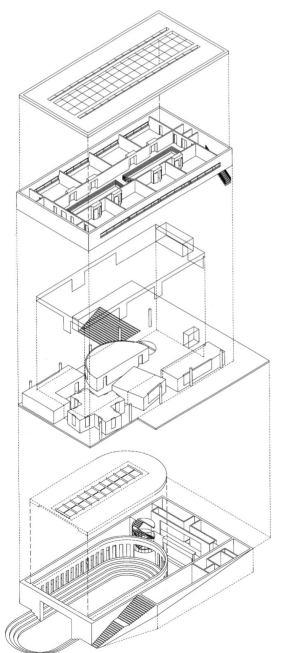

those of today is the building and site configuration: most have only one entrance, and the spaces between the buildings where children are most often traversing have been reduced.

SPECIAL SCHOOLS AND MATERIALS

This volume also covers a selection of specialised private schools, such as a music school for musically gifted children by Valentyn and Oreyzi and a Jewish primary school in Berlin by Zvi Hecker. On a different tangent are the Waldorf or Steiner schools by plus+ bauplanung and Arbeidsgruppen HUS.

Although these schools are not directly comparable in every sense to the non-specialised schools, there are some areas where they overlap. But more than this they represent an alternative approach to school building. Mostly because these schools are privately funded, but also due to their speciality, the selection and use of materials for these projects is sometimes more 'luxurious' than is usual. For their Musikgymnasiums Schloß Belvedere bei Weimar (Music High School in Weimar) in Germany, Valentyn and Oreyzi used wood as wall-panelling as well as for the floors (it was necessary for this design to adhere to specific acoustic standards), shipbuilders' plywood for the facade of some of the rooms, and a generous amount of glass.

Zvi Hecker's design for the Jewish Primary School in Berlin uses ordinary economical materials – concrete, brick and corrugated metal cladding – but in a most unusual plan. The school unfolds like a flower, its 'streets' and 'paths' following the orbits of the sun.

The two Steiner schools (or Waldorf schools) in this volume follow the principles for school buildings as laid down by Rudolf Steiner (1861–1925). Steiner established the philosophy of education known as 'anthroposophy', which emphasised the importance of arts and social interaction in a child's education and encouraged a very free and natural development for the child. The first Steiner school was built by Steiner himself in Stuttgart, Germany, in 1919. Both Steiner projects presented here are difficult to describe adequately with words – suffice to say there is a sense of a freeform or organic unfolding to the plans. None of the classrooms take regular form; they are instead polygonal and open in character. For example, Arbeidsgruppen's Steiner School in Stavanger, Norway, is characterised by a series of hyperbolic roofs and domes that pull and push all ways at the same time.

CONCLUSION

What is typically seen as a problem in school design – that the educationalists are continually changing their needs – should be turned around as a welcome challenge for architects. The challenge is to find a flexible design solution, and by virtue of the fact that it is a flexible space as opposed to static and not changeable, the design is likely to be unique, with the ability to evolve with its users. As children learn and grow, so should the buildings around them.

TALKS WITH:

Ray C Bordwell, Principal Partner at Perkins & Will

Steve Clow, Head of Architecture at Hampshire County Council Architects

Nev Churcher, Architect of Woodlea and Whiteley Primary Schools, Hampshire County Council Architects

PERKINS & WILL

Perkins & Will, founded in Chicago in 1935, with eight offices, and over 500 design professionals working under its name, has completed projects in 37 countries. The architects first gained international recognition in the 1930s for their design of educational facilities, starting with the 1938 Crow Island School. Since then they have designed and built hundreds of school, college and university projects throughout the world.

In the 1950s, design of healthcare facilities became an equally significant part of the practice: they have completed over 300 medical institutions in the US to date. The corporate-commercial practice of the firm developed in the 1960s, and includes R&D facilities to offices and banks. The firm has received hundreds of awards and was named American Institute of Architects Firm of the Year for 1999.

Ray C Bordwell, Principal Partner, is a name associated with school design. His views on architecture in education are respected throughout the world.

Having worked on so many school projects to date, has the firm now established a working methodology for designing schools or is each project very different?

RCB: Each school is different and deserves special attention. One design solution does not fit every need. In the US, the vision of a sprawling suburban campus on hundreds of acres of wooded land conjures up images quite different from those of an urban school on four city blocks. Apart from the contextual differences there are social, demographic and economic influences that can dramatically shape facility design. For example, a school in an economically deprived neighbourhood may need to serve breakfast and provide expanded healthcare facilities. The numbers and type of counselling services and occupational education are a few others.

In the case of designing both new and renovated facilities, the process is built on a workshop format and is a collaborative exercise undertaken over many weeks. Involving several groups of users it is designed to explore the current and future needs of the building while learning from past performance using a 'research'-based approach – in other words, knowing what the decisions you make are based on.

Although several firms and independent organisations undertake a similar process, I believe Perkins & Will's has some distinct differences and advantages.

Our process combines a process-driven workshop to develop background information on the district's educational needs (often referred to as an 'Ed Spec') with architectural programming that specifically defines spatial and relational needs of the physical space.

During the workshops we explore new ideas of programme delivery and look to the administrators, staff, students and community members to fuel innovation. The results of this phase are a clear definition of the types of spaces necessary, their intended use and their relationship with each other. We also address issues of sustainable design, technology integration, safety and security as part of the collaboration. Combining these findings with a series of defined architectural parameters such as budget, code, site and time schedules completes the picture and is the content of what we publish as the final deliverable. This 'Facilities Design Guideline', unlike many Ed Specs, closes the 'disconnection' that can occur between the facility programming and the design architect's directive. It 'closes' the loop on often-troublesome issues that are left for the design architect to determine. The document is very graphic in its representation of information, so the 'visually thinking' architect can make an immediate connection to the information. With this approach there are fewer misunderstandings on the part of both parties.

Does Perkins & Will have a 'green' policy in its approach to school design?

RCB: Our policy, if you will, is cultural more than anything in our educational practice. It is something that we just 'do'. There are, however, six topics of sustainable design that we address in every project, many of which have a direct impact on student performance:

- **Reductions in Energy Costs** An early focus on energy performance and the use of sophisticated energy analysis software to optimise anticipated energy performance while maintaining a high degree of comfort and control.
- **Day lighting** Careful site analysis and solar orientation maximising opportunities to use natural light for illumination, for reducing energy costs, and for taking advantage of the direct link between daylighting and school performance.
- **Improving Indoor Environmental Quality** Substantial improvements to the air quality of indoor environments is essential in reducing long-term risks to human health
- **Maximising Landscape and Site Design** Using native plant materials and absorption drainage to increase biodiversity and improve surface water quality, minimising maintenance costs.
- **Conserving Natural Resources** Careful selection of materials helps reduce the draw-down of finite resources and reduces construction waste. This also encourages the development of alternative material industries.

- **Sustainability as a teaching tool** In addition to preserving the environment, green buildings also preserve the future of the environment by educating today's youth on the impact of their actions on the environment.

How do urban versus rural projects most differ in design and design method?

RCB: Issues of economic and demographic variation from one area to another can be major factors in urban districts.

In rural schools, if you are building a new high school, it may be the only high school in the entire district. In some ways this is the easiest of all projects. The community and educational values are easier to identify so it is quite likely that you will have a basic agreement on the needs of the facility. Apart from the land issues, urban districts may have several high schools – New York City has dozens. They also had a 20 per cent dropout rate in 2001.

In urban districts, there might be several different types of schools, each with a different focus. These can include vocational/technical, science, academic/comprehensive, alternative and several variations on each.

How significant is the size of the school, especially with regard to the overall architectural plans?

RCB: Designing a smaller school can be challenging if trying to maintain the same guidelines for 'square-feet-per-student'. For example, consider two schools – one for 2,000 students and the other for 300 students. Each school has a gymnasium. Now, here is the hard part. Most districts place guidelines on the facilities for size. In this example, the area limitation will be 163 square feet (15 square metres) allowed for each student. The gymnasium, because it has a basketball court, is the same size in each. In other words, there are fewer students in the small school to amortise the gymnasium area than there are in the large school. Statistically, this means that, in general, as the number of students goes down, the square-feet-per-student goes up. This is both the challenge and the opportunity. We now have a few small schools underway, and these are very exciting in terms of planning innovations.

Is the concept of 'school as a village' something you support and aim to achieve when designing larger schools?

RCB: It's called many things but, generally, yes. Building smaller schools within the larger school has many benefits. These smaller communities can foster a better relationship between students and staff, reduce security problems by limiting student movement around the larger building, and provide zoning opportunities so that portions of the building can remain open later at night or at weekends, and so on.

How important is the participation of the end-users of the school in the design process?

RCB: See the answer to the first question. Not only is it feasible but necessary, and I find it to be the most exciting part of the project. It's where all the big ideas come from, and is also the foundation of innovation.

How do you measure the success of your school buildings? What makes one type of school design better than another?

RCB: Success can be measured in a number of ways, including user satisfaction, community support, improved test scores, reduced operational cost, etc.

From an instructional point of view, I believe there are two components or basic units of measuring the success of an educational facility. These are flexibility/agility of the final structure, and the ability of the classroom to meet programme needs.

On the flexibility point, many existing school construction methods and classroom configurations make later changes cost-prohibitive and difficult to accomplish. Given the ever-changing needs of students, schools and the new economy, facilities need to be built so that change is welcomed, not thwarted. Building materials and furniture should be selected to support the variety of learning opportunities found in today's student-centred model of instruction. This means that all elements of a school facility should be designed to support the reconfigurations deemed necessary for future learning.

In addressing the classroom issue, it is much more important issue than you and I might envision, and includes the support spaces that go with them. Areas like small group-rooms, teacher offices, workrooms and storage space all combine to support the 'classroom of the twenty-first century'. Really it is a 'learning environment' more than a classroom.

Given the workforce and economic trends, students today (and in the foreseeable future) need a high degree of competency in problem-solving, leadership and communication skills utilised in a 'team-based' workforce. These requirements put new pressure on educational facilities to satisfy the need for educational space beyond the traditional 'place where classes meet'. School buildings have evolved beyond just classrooms to become 'learning environments', or places where teaching and learning occur in a variety of settings that utilise a vast array of support technology. Learning can, and will, take place in classrooms, but it also takes place in hallways, cafeterias, conference rooms, gymnasiums and (in many cases) at remote sites. This definition of a learning environment expands our definition of a school from a factory model to 'a place where the space, circumstances, objects and conditions surround the act or experience of learning'.

If this is the thinking from the very beginning of a project, then the criteria necessary for evaluating the success of a facility's ability to meet student, staff and community needs will be self-evident.

HAMPSHIRE COUNTY COUNCIL ARCHITECTS

Hampshire County Council Architects was established in 1974. The office employs over 250 professional, technical and support staff. It offers architectural design, landscape design, interior design, graphic design, project development, environmental, mechanical and electrical engineering services, structural engineering and quantity surveying. The office has been responsible for a variety of school buildings, libraries, offices, social services properties and museums. Hampshire County Council Architects have won many awards for their school buildings, including the Royal Institute of British Architects (RIBA) National and Regional Awards, and in 1991 the Gold Medal Award to Colin Stansfield-Smith, then Head of Architecture.

Steve Clow, Head of Architecture, joined Hampshire in 1987 and has been the Head of Architecture since 1998. He designed the Berrywood Primary School in Hedge End which won the RIBA Regional award 1990.

He also designed Hackney Community College which won the RIBA Regional Award and the Fine Art Commission Award for integration of art in buildings. Here he talks about the development of the office and Hampshire's approach to designing school buildings, including Woodlea and Queens Inclosure, both of which are featured in this volume.

Briefly, how have Hampshire County Council Architects come to be known as specialists in school design?

SC: During 1974, local government reorganisation led to a newly appointed county architect and a new leader for Hampshire County Council who was passionate about community architecture. This fortunate combination resulted in the creation of new buildings. The architectural department then grew and attracted talented designers and architects, some of them fresh out of college.

The then Head of Architecture, Colin Stansfield-Smith, wanted to introduce architecture that related to the site. (Prior to this Hampshire had built prefabricated buildings with standard flat roofs that were not sensitive to the site.)

Throughout the 1980s, Hampshire were building schools that were site specific, with themes to the design; for example, large barn-like spaces that were naturally lit. The brief for each school was the same, but the results were very different. Variety came into design rather than simply one standard solution for the same brief, and these schools came to be recognised by the architectural press and raised our practice to a higher level.

Do you have a green policy in your approach to school design?

SC: We have a policy of sustainability. Our architecture explores design and construction in a sustainable manner. We also have a county council which is pursuing green policies. We are experimenting with materials but avoid things like solvents in paints, and instead use water-based paints. It is still early days. Natural ventilation is easy and green, and has been used for years. However, what might be economical and sustainable may not be green: for example, nylon carpets are cheap and hardwearing but not green.

Other sustainable design includes moving away from painting jobs and instead using aluminium systems that do not need repainting, and roofing systems that are very hardwearing – to reduce high maintenance costs. We consider the economy of maintenance: school money is mostly spent on heating, lighting, mechanical and electrical systems, so we build with high insulation and optimise daylight to keep the costs down.

Do you have a general working methodology towards school design, or do you approach each project as new?

SC: We approach every site with a fresh mind and take on board the context. If it is a new school campus then it is easier; if it is an extension to an existing site we try to retain the character of the original site in our designs.

Woodlea Primary School was a site that was completely wooded. We had to cut down some trees to fit it in. We then used the wood in the school building. The site is also very steep and so the building sits out of the ground. The school is one building but expressed as a series of roofs; so rather than seeing one big building, it reads as a series of buildings linked together, defined by many roofs. There are seven classrooms at Woodlea.

The Queens Inclosure Primary School site, by comparison, was an open field by woodland. We did not have to cut down trees. It was a very different design solution though the brief was the same as that for Woodlea. We used glass and steel so that the building became transparent, and opened one edge to this enclosure so it was linked to the outside. The building is basically two barrel vault roofs and glass. The costs were similar to Woodlea despite the different types of architecture.

Is colour an important part of your design for schools?

SC: Colour is vital. We have an interior designer who contributes at this stage, and we also involve the end-user regarding school colours and selection of furniture. In addition we have become involved in school art projects; for example, the curtains in the hall became cloth painted by the students, and the floor tiles were designed by children (Woodlea).

Twenty years ago it was popular to use primary colours but these can get very tired. Today we are using more muted, natural-looking colours, and often plain white or off-white backgrounds.

Stakes Hill Infant School

Queens Inclosure Primary School

How does the size of the school affect your design?

SC: The constraints of the site might make the project difficult if it is a small site and a large building. The challenge becomes the context. Primary school briefs are all the same, for around 420 pupils (two forms of entry). Secondary schools are much more complex – with science labs, a gym, theatres, etc. Size is less of a challenge than the context. The largest school we have designed from scratch is for 950 students. However, we have worked on extensions for schools with up to 2,000 students.

Is it important to involve the end-users of the school in the design process?

SC: It is crucial that we work with head teachers and governors who will then involve teachers and parents, and perhaps pupils. We do this through meetings. It is easier to establish the brief with the user if it is an existing building. If it is a new school and no head teacher has been appointed, there is less involvement.

We get feedback through questionnaires. About 85 per cent think our schools are good or excellent. The most powerful comments have come from those moving out of old facilities into new facilities.

On a more personal note, what are your favourite aspects of school building?

SC: I get the most satisfaction from the building being used, for example the children and teaching staff enjoying the space. I am also very happy to be introducing the new use of green materials.

Nev Churcher, Architect with Hampshire County Council Architects, designed both Woodlea and Whiteley Primary Schools, both of which have been awarded RIBA National Awards, in 1993 and 2002 respectively. Here he talks about Woodlea Primary School, and schools as a total learning environment.

NC: When designing for little children, the organisation needs to be explicit. It is a different environment for them. Here, the children have the opportunity to learn about real spaces. They are at school and not at home, and they need to realise this through explicit design – explicit in terms of materials used. For example, where we used metal (a non-green material) we have left it as is rather than painting it, to show what it is. And in fact, using metal in this instance is more green than using wood that would need to be replaced year after year.

How do you measure the success of the architecture? It is architecture, but it is the end-user who defines its success through use. When we finished the school (Woodlea) and the work was over, I felt as though I had nothing to do with it. The school took off with a life of its own. The users (teachers and children) moved things around according to need, and exchanged other things. There was such a feeling of calm and well-being. It was amazing.

Most important is the need to produce a sense of 'place' and inevitability – and places with as rich a mix as possible – a total learning environment, where natural and created elements are in harmony. All the main spaces at Whiteley are naturally lit and ventilated during a normal school day, which benefits the users and the health of the planet (electricity bills are 35 per cent of the norm). Deciduous tress are used close to the buildings as natural environmental control devices; leafy shade in the summer, skeletons to allow in low-angle sun in the winter – cheap and beautiful.

The natural 'bowl' in the landscape of Woodlea very much influenced the design of the school. Despite the site spanning a one-in-seven slope, we managed to spread the buildings out over three levels accessed by ramps. The plan has twenty dimensions to it. It is like a little village of things.

The design and realisation of the schools (Woodlea and Whiteley) has continued an all-embracing, people-based approach that aims to produce places to educate young people – places that are beautiful but practical, stimulating yet calm, energy efficient and sustainable.

Buildings, especially dwellings and schools, should be an education in themselves

Woodlea Primary School

Woodlea Primary School

Allford Hall Monaghan Morris (AHMM)
GREAT NOTLEY PRIMARY SCHOOL

Essex, England

Great Notley Primary School is the result of an international competition for a model school that demonstrates sustainable principles within a standard UK Department for Education (DfEE) budget of £1.25 million. The team, led by Allford Hall Monaghan Morris (AHMM), was chosen on the basis of their experience in school design in June 1997 to develop the scheme for a fixed opening date for in September 1999.

The aim of the competition was threefold: to produce a high-quality new school to a standard government budget; to establish the principles of a sustainable building and method of construction; and to record the process of designing and constructing the product.

As lead consultants, AHMM worked in close liaison with the consultant team, including artists (funded by a Royal Society of Arts grant attending design team meetings) and the client (itself an expert in schools). The initial investigation involved the production of a series of study models of possible layouts and options, which were assessed on the key criteria of quality, cost and sustainability. The triangular model form was one of four 'generic' solutions discussed, modelled and tested by the team, and emerged as the clearly preferred design option.

The school, a single-storey triangular-shaped building, provides generous classroom spaces by rationalising circulation. Its distinctive triangular shape is most striking, having the advantage in wall-to-floor ratio and many possibilities in terms of arranging internal spaces. The six classrooms edge one side of the triangle, and all other spaces are organised around a central inner court. Circulation space has been restricted to one corridor, reducing the area and freeing up some cash for reinvesting in other areas. The inner court, which originally started out as an external court on the plan, and the 'nose' of the triangle, which serves as a covered external teaching area, were both 'bonus' spaces, surplus to the requirements of the brief.

In terms of sustainability, natural ventilation and light are provided through a simple low-energy enclosure. All materials and the site itself were carefully assessed in terms of their use and recyclable potential. As a result of this research, numerous recycled, low-embodied energy and environmentally preferred products have been utilised in the project.

The design process was required to involve the public and the end-user, as dictated by the brief. This was difficult as the school was to serve a community that did not yet exist. Instead, a mock-user group was used, made up from heads and teachers from other schools. Throughout the design process, feedback was given from the public through public exhibitions at both professionally related and public venues.

The architects viewed sustainability as: 'a tag that can be too glibly attached by the professions to new projects; we accepted that the selection of materials was dependent on a subjective assessment of the following criteria: recyclability, embodied energy, energy in use, lifecycle costings, maintenance and quality. As a result we can openly admit that there is a certain irony to the fact that despite clear justification we confirm that the windows are from Sweden, the roof from Germany and the floors are from China'.

Nevertheless, the project has been selected as a demonstration project for both sustainability and technology.

Awards
The school has been awarded a RIBA Award for Architecture and Millennium Product Status. In June 2000 it received the Royal Fine Arts Commission Award for education buildings.

Perspective view

Left Perspective view

Below Site plan

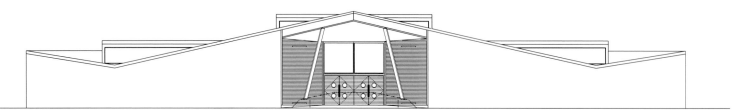

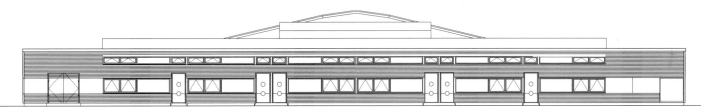

Opposite top The 'nose' of the school that is also used as a covered outdoor teaching area

Opposite bottom North elevation

Top Wide view of the school with coloured doors

Centre South elevation

Bottom Side of the school detailing 'green' roof

Above Perspective view

Right Ground floor plan

Opposite The doors are identified by colour

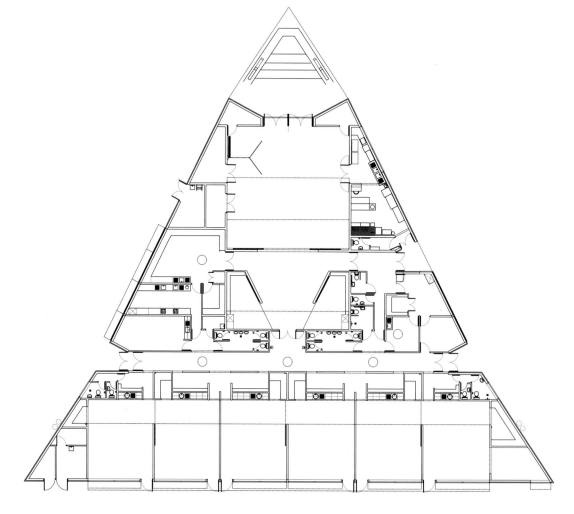

School Builders

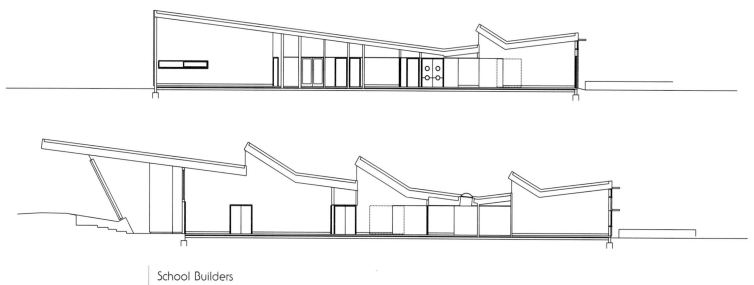

Opposite top Long view of the school

Opposite centre Long section through kitchen to classroom

Opposite bottom Long section through hall to classroom

Above Children playing outside

Right Detail of surface in classroom

Below Children in class

Opposite The inner court and hall are linked with sliding doors

STEINERSKOLEN I STAVANGER (STEINER SCHOOL STAVANGER)

Stavanger, Norway

The site is peripheral, among a rather regimented suburb, to which the new building is in dramatic contrast. At first, it seems to be some sort of strange and ancient structure transplanted out of the depth of the primeval forests to its decorous, sanitised late 20th-century location. Closer inspection reveals, for instance, that the use of glass must make it a building of the last hundred years or so...
(*Architectural Review,* Norway Special Issue, August 1996.)

The first stages of planning for the Steinerskolen in Stavanger took place in 1988. Six buildings have since been completed, although this represents just 60 per cent of the school.

The buildings are characterised by double-curved hyperbolic-parabolic roofs, a form that expresses two shapes simultaneously. These bow down and embrace the classrooms at the middle wall of the building, while at the same time swinging towards the sky and pointing upwards and outwards at the outer walls, embodying Rudolf Steiner's pedagogic principles of being open and welcoming, and stimulating students to be open to new knowledge, skills and experiences.

The main entrance to the building is on the upper floor, across a curving wooden bridge. Here a curved void opens down to the hall, which is the main communal space of the building. Classrooms are on the upper floor with curved hyperbolic ceilings, and are filled with natural light from the skylights. On the lower floor are the workshops with warm pine walls and large windows to afford a good amount of natural light.

There are two exceptions to the hyperbolic roofs in the school complex: at two points the duality of the roofing is replaced by domes. Indeed, the main dome of the school is yet to be built, and will hold the centre of gravity for the whole school. The domed roofs consist of steel primary construction with ventilated timber construction in between. All the roofs are covered with used slate gathered from the surrounding districts, and this is small enough to follow the complex curves of the roof, and open enough to allow air to circulate.

The walls are 'breathable' to avoid condensation and other humidity problems in such a cold northern climate. The outer layer is made of permeable rough boarding, the inner cladding of timber or board then the insulation (all external walls and roofs have been injected with cellulose fibre insulation) and finally the inner finishings.

The interior walls of the middle part consist of rendered block facade and brick, and in the domes, timber stud construction. Internal partitions are of plasterboard and timber panelling. Ceilings consist of cement wood fibreboard while the floor is linoleum, ceramic tiles and timber parquet. Externals walls are timber stud construction, and the vertical timber panelling is in various thicknesses and widths, in plywood and rendered block and brickwork.

Arbeidsgruppen worked with specialists Norske Skog to evolve approaches to healthy wood treatment, and as a result all woods have been treated with non-toxic varnishes, including traditional remedies such as oil or beeswax lacquers.

Model of finished school

Above Glass and wood panelled facade
with connecting bridge to upper level

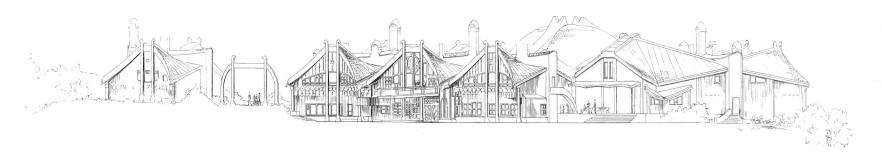

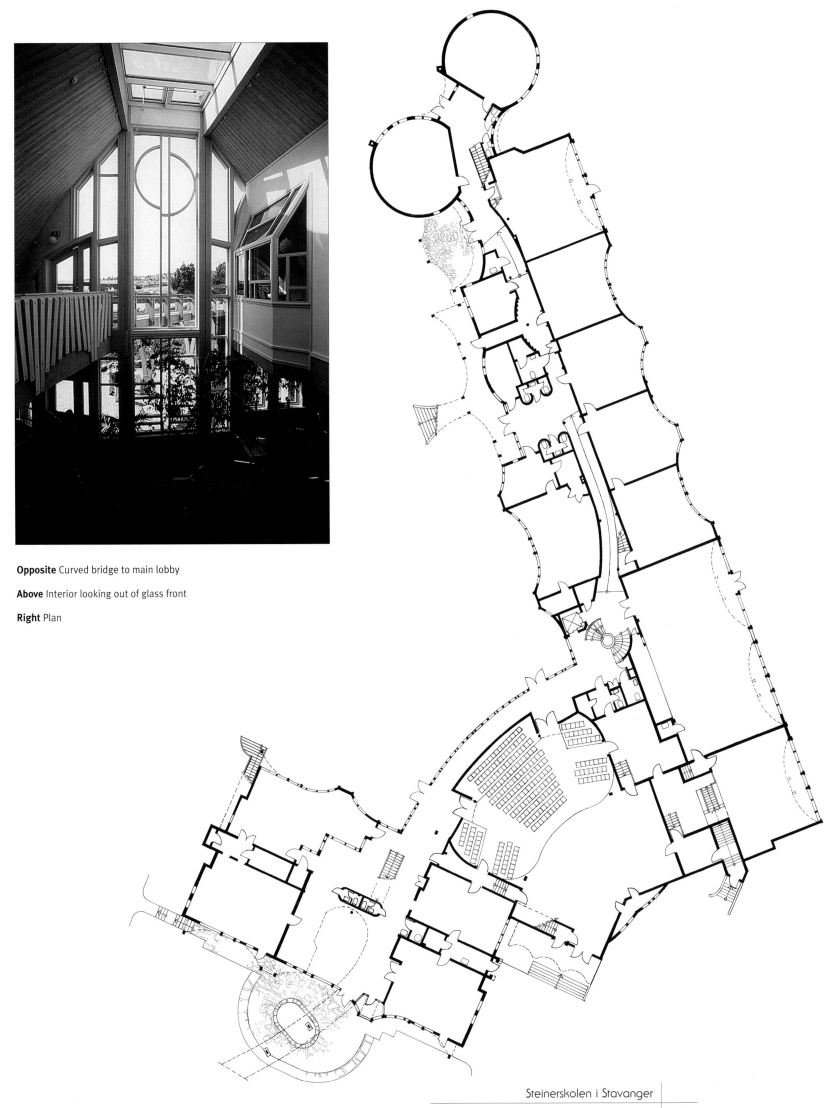

Opposite Curved bridge to main lobby

Above Interior looking out of glass front

Right Plan

Steinerskolen i Stavanger

Above Walkway to classrooms

Below View from east

Opposite Detail of wood facade

Steinerskolen i Stavanger

Above View from west

Opposite Exterior of class-rooms showing slated roof

Right View of school at dusk

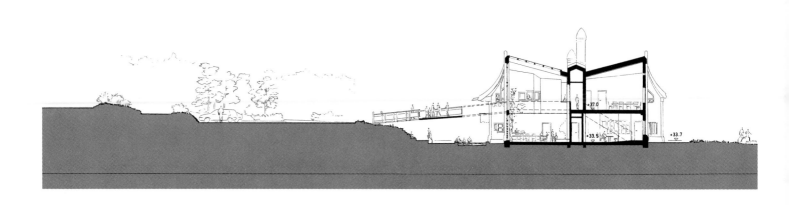

Opposite top Section

Opposite bottom Interior of classroom
with curved ceiling up towards skylights

Above Interior of classroom showing
domed ceiling

Right Section

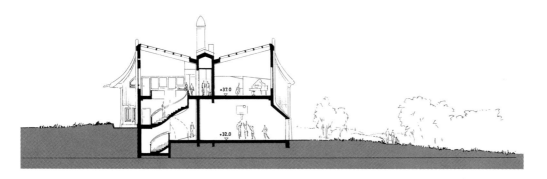

Steinerskolen i Stavanger

HAUTE VALLÉE SCHOOL

Jersey, Channel Islands, England

Haute Vallée School is a series of shapes and forms set among a very unusual curved and geometric plan. The school buildings are organised around a north–south curved grid broken by a single diagonal 'street' running through the building forms, which also marks the entrance route. The diagonal line also serves to divide those buildings used only by the school and those shared by the local community.

The shapes and forms of the various buildings are enhanced by the natural slope of the site; the changes of level are bridged by various pedestrian links and the overall result is more akin to an urban centre with streets, walkways, courtyards and a central amphitheatre-styled piazza. The campus is an assembly of functional clusters – classrooms, a science block, music and administration rooms, a library and technology centre, hall/theatre and a sports complex with a swimming pool.

The curved classroom block is oriented on the north side, affording shade from the sun, with the cool north and warm south sides of the curve offering good ventilation (boosted by ventilation chimneys protruding down through the ceiling). External and internal blinds are used to control solar heat gain, allowing daylight without glare, and the landscape has been designed to offer more shade with deciduous trees planted on the south side.

The piazza is the heart of the school and hosts a circular granite-clad stair tower marking the entrance to the glazed dining block, also the front to the main school hall. The hall is designed as a flexible space – a 350-seater theatre with dining facilities for evening activities, conferences or local theatre groups. On the south side of the main piazza, a vibrant blue concrete wall with an inverted canopy roof fits between the administration and library buildings, giving a powerful visual reference.

Specialist consultants were involved in the development of the environmental strategy of the building in order to meet the client's brief that the school be as highly energy-efficient as possible.

Opposite top: Entrance to theatre with stair tower to the left

Opposite bottom: Front facade of classrooms

Left: Interior of gym

Right: Granite clad stair tower marking entrance to dining block

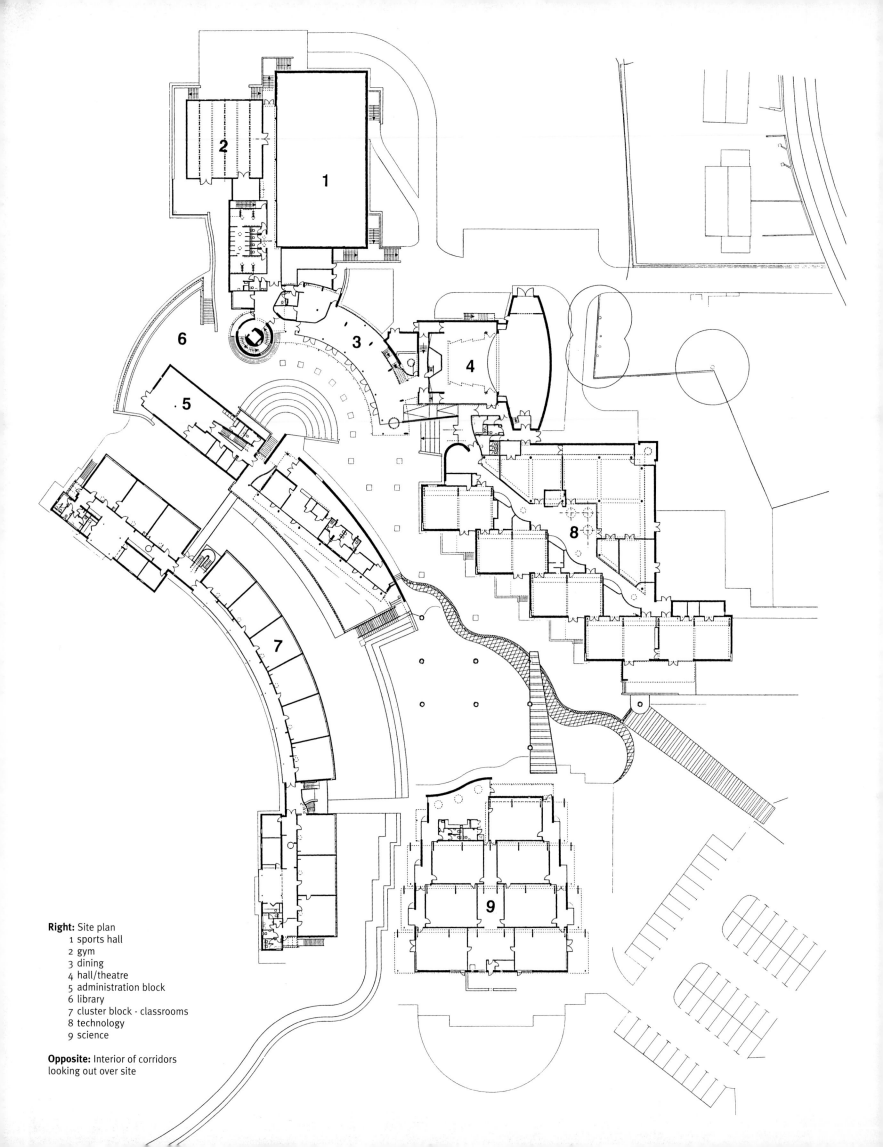

Right: Site plan
1 sports hall
2 gym
3 dining
4 hall/theatre
5 administration block
6 library
7 cluster block - classrooms
8 technology
9 science

Opposite: Interior of corridors
looking out over site

Above: Classroom interior

Below: Section

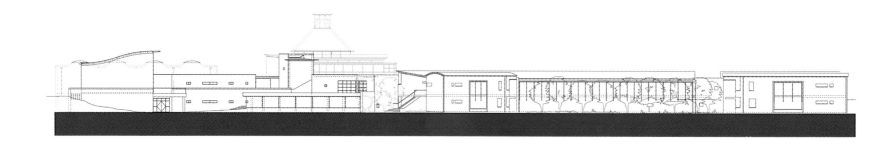

Library interior

DRUK WHITE LOTUS SCHOOL

The Druk White Lotus School project is an initiative of the Drukpa Trust, a UK-registered charity, and is under the patronage of HH the Dalai Lama. The aim of the project is to build and sustain a new school for 800 mixed pupils in the village of Shey, Ladakh, in the western Himalayas of northern India.

The school will offer a model academic curriculum combined with the needs of the local community, within a culture under enormous pressure to change. The school will allow the children to be taught in the local language – Ladakkhi – and the local culture – Buddhism. (Many Indian schoolchildren are taught and examined in English.)

The plan and design of the school uses Tibetan Buddhist symbols: it is a circular form with nine square arrangements (or courtyards), called a *mandala* (symbolising the universe). Each courtyard has cost approximately £100,000 (including infrastructure), estimated to be one-tenth of what it might cost in Europe.

The first phase opened for teaching in September 2001 and includes the nursery and infant school courtyard, solar energy centre and water infrastructure as part of the ongoing construction programme. It accommodates 80 children. The larger masterplan, to be phased over eight years and due for completion in 2010, includes further teaching courtyards, vocational training workshops, an open-air temple, dining hall and kitchens, computer and science labs, art studios, a medical clinic and residential accommodation for some pupils and staff. The school will eventually accommodate 800 children.

This has been a very different project for Arup, involving high-level analysis to solve problems using traditional materials: for example analysing seismic performance, solar energy passive heating and cooling, and water recycling. The whole project is conceived as a model for appropriate and sustainable modernisation in Ladakh, providing a high quality of environment for teaching and supporting the living community of the school. The desert site will be entirely self-regulating in terms of water cycle, and all buildings will take maximum advantage of the high-altitude climate.

The spaces and their structures are designed for flexibility, excellent daylighting and ventilation, active or passive solar energy collection (no energy is imported, and there are solar-assisted ventilated improved pit (VIP) latrines), and to perform safely during earthquakes. Building materials are mostly indigenous to Ladakh, with careful auditing of sustainable resource supply. Local expertise, in terms of detailing and the symbolic aspects of the architecture, is also a fundamental to the design.

(Arup is a patron to the UK charity REDR (Register of Engineers for Disaster Relief) which registers people who are trained and prepared to go to areas where there is a need for engineering skills.)

Opposite top View of school with dramatic mountainous backdrop

Opposite bottom Detailed view of school from courtyard

Above View of school courtyard

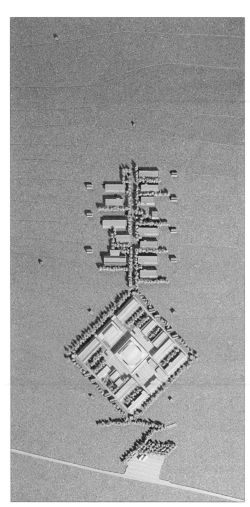

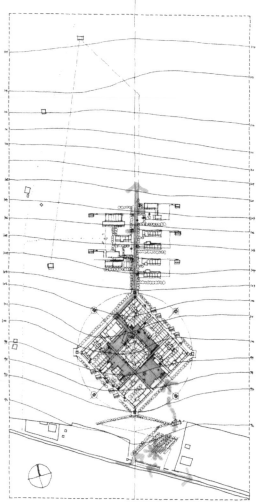

Far left Model of school, aerial view

Left Site plan

Below left Floor plan
1 Entrance to courtyard
2 External teaching spaces
3 Water point and play
4 Nursery
5 Lower kindergarten
6 Upper kindergarten
7 Year 1
8 Teacher/administration spaces
9 Solar assisted VIP latrines
10 Air lock and lockers
11 Warm/quiet corner

Bottom left Section

Opposite top Interior of classroom filled with natural light

Opposite bottom Detail of wooden construction of classrooms and stone walls

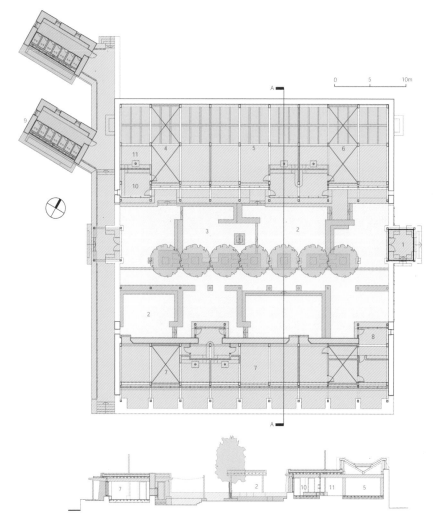

Classroom building with plants on the roof

MONTESSORI SCHOOL INGOLSTADT

Hollerstauden, Germany

The site for the new school at Ingolstadt was relatively large, bordering green areas and an existing kindergarten of the local parish. Rather than one large building, it consists of five smaller buildings. On entering there is a semi-public main building, followed by the kindergarten, a building for therapy, the primary school and finally the modern secondary school with workshops and a meeting place.

Individual buildings are grouped around a central green area, linking the 'inside' of the site with the 'outside' of the bordering green area. The 'green' classrooms and common rooms have wooden decks out front, which are further protected by hedges and high shrubs, allowing classes to be held outside if weather permits. Each classroom has its own special tree, which makes it individual and also affords some shade.

It was at the request of the client that the ground plan of the upper storeys should take on the form of a simple geometric design, this could be for example a circle, a square or an equilateral triangle. Failing this these upper storeys would tower over the rest of the one-storey complex. In this way the shapes corresponded to the overall project and help to give the complex its identity.

'Before we started to develop this project, members of the foundation and the architects visited existing Montessori schools. We were particularly interested in two complexes in Holland, which had been planned by the architect Hermann Hertzberger. We were impressed with his buildings and by the relaxed live characteristics of the school itself. Many ideas of these these two buildings we carried over: the nondirectional, open, diverse classroom zones are not merely classrooms; the interior is closely related to the exterior, and elements of the surrounding gardens, to the plants, squares, and to the many different kinds of light... And some new elements were added; they were developed together with the school.

According to Günter Behnisch: 'What you get are buildings, each with their own emphasis. Regarding their exterior, they are similar to each other, as they share some common features – the same window types, roof projections, panelling, etc, and all together form the school complex. Inside, however, every building has its own character, its own geometry – a special-shaped hall, differently constructed staircases, its own lighting mood. Each of these interior spaces suggests a particular kind of use in correspondence to its special task'.

Panoramic view of site

Above left Classroom building with circular first floor

Above right Classroom building

Right Plan
1 Community centre
  Management
  Kitchen/Canteen
  Seminar room
2 Secondary school
  11 classrooms
3 Primary school
  13 classrooms
4 Kindergarten
5 Therapy rooms

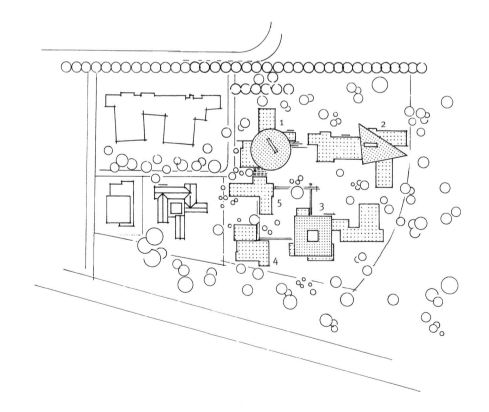

Composite plan

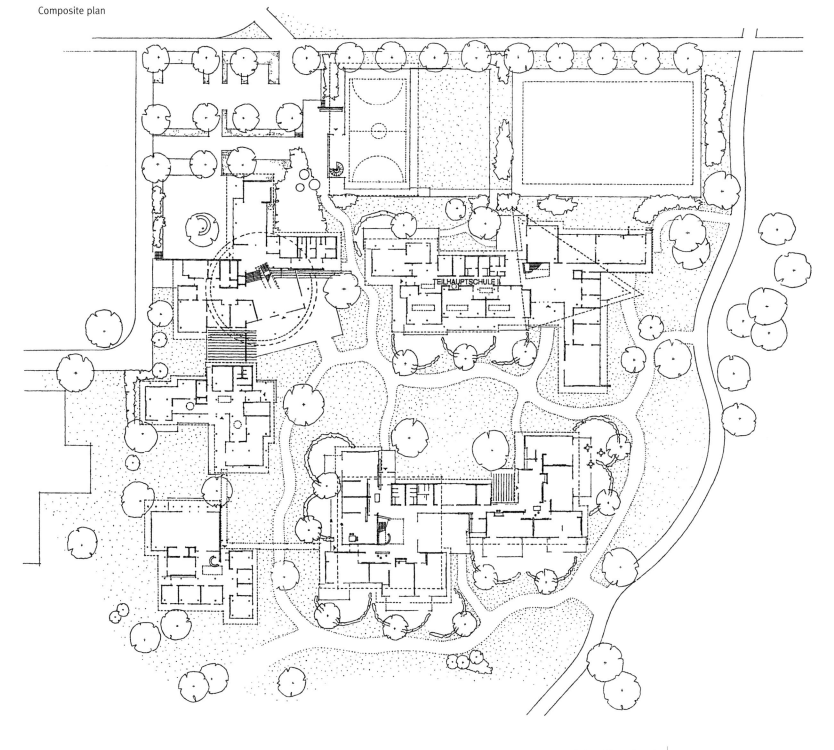

TEILHAUPTSCHULE II

Top Panoramic view of inner courtyard

Bottom Sections

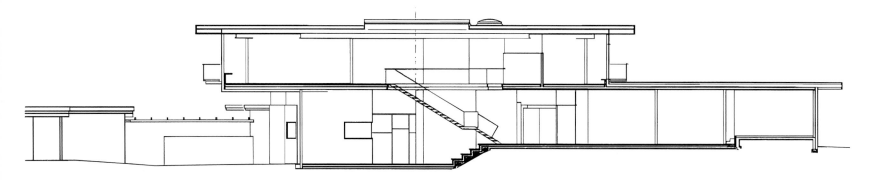

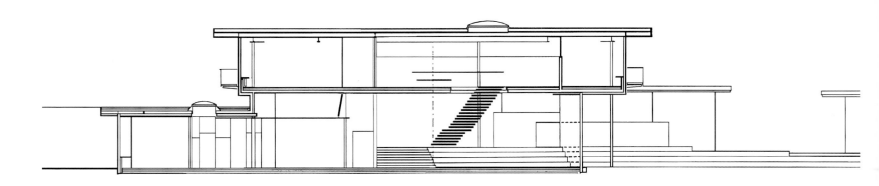

Opposite top left Upper level of school

Opposite top right Interior of corridor

Below Interior leading out to courtyard

Montessori School Ingolstadt

Interior of classroom

Interior of cloakroom

Coloured walls in classroom hallway

VOCATIONAL SCHOOL

This new school complex in the Hohenlohe region of Öhringen was based on a design that received first prize in an open competition. The site lies in a valley formed by the Öhrn river, and is typical of an area on the outskirts of a town – with an elevated autobahn nearby, a shopping centre, several industrial buildings and some residences.

Behnisch and Partner decided to give the new school a powerful and self-sufficient identity that would give character to the area: 'In this rather heterogeneous situation, which is easy to confuse with almost identical situations in many other towns, we were unable to find any feature from which the appearance of the professional school could be derived. We therefore decided to develop a relatively independent design which would on its own be able to shape the character of the particular location'.

The school is a two-storey broken ring elevated on columns, swooping towards and away from the autobahn. A larger gymnasium lies between the autobahn and the school building. The relatively high water table also encouraged the structure to move upwards, and led to extensive landscaping of the site.

The classrooms on the outer layer of the ring look outward; the inner layer of the ring is lined with stairs, hallways, ancillary rooms and a large three-level hall. The hall is the centre of the school and is used for meetings, performances and socialising. It is big enough to house the entire school.

'Without doubt a shape as egocentric as that of a circle tends to impose its laws on the subordinate elements and shapes. Naturally we have put great effort into finding ways of dealing with such constraints; this is expressed in the design. In the end, we came to realise that even the fully glazed facade addressing the interior courtyard tended to "close itself" - it was intended to appear as a glazed gallery. We therefore asked artist Erich Wiesner to assist us. He was charged with the task of visually "dissolving" the glazed envelope by applying bold colours to the walls between the classrooms and the corridor, a challenge with a successful conclusion', say the architects.

'With this building, as with others in the past, we found that outside creative influence in the end enriched our work, driving us to design something much more dynamic and more unusual than what we alone could have produced'.

Panoramic view of school

Left Outer ring of school

Below Site plan

Upper floor external detail

Above Inner ring with housed staircase

Opposite right Internal classroom hallway

Opposite far right Coloured walls in
classroom hallway

Inner court

Left View from hallway on to inner court

Below Plan

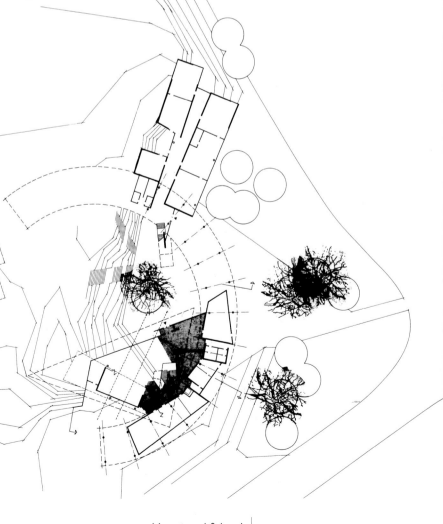

Meeting space in main building

Stairways to upper levels

HAMPDEN GURNEY SCHOOL

London, England

The new Hampden Gurney School replaces a one- and two-storey building on a Second World War bomb site, and is the result of a competition by the school trustees. As a Church of England school that prides itself on its high academic standards, Hampden Gurney had for a number of years sought to improve its premises in a way that would also satisfy the educational demands of the twenty-first century.

The 'vertical school' design idea sets the school as the cornerpiece of a recreated Marylebone city-block, overlooking the constant activity of London's busy Edgware Road nearby. The building, on the prominent southwest corner, forms an internal courtyard with two new interrelated residential street buildings.

The conspicuous location also gives the school the best aspect for sunlight. The deliberately outward-looking building recognises the trustees' aspirations for it to play an active role in the social life of the community. Created on six levels, it has a physical presence among its high neighbouring buildings, giving staff and pupils a new prospect over their surroundings.

The classrooms are set on three levels above ground floor, together with the library and the multimedia room, and there is a group teaching room on the roof. Adjacent to the classrooms are open-air play decks that are weather proof and safe. (These can also double as open-air classrooms on warm days.) All teaching rooms enjoy good north light and have the prospect over the courtyard garden formed by the residential buildings. The hall, chapel, and music and drama room are set at the lower ground level (one level below the pavement).

A new nursery for thirty children is located at ground level, which is set 900 millimetres (35.4 inches) above the level of the existing pavement. Two generous ramps and steps give easy access to the school entrances for small children and parents with prams.

Play areas have been located at each level of teaching, separated from the classrooms by a bridge across the central lightwell. The play areas are open to the fresh air and the long side of each is curved to the south to enjoy an all-day-long sun path. The lower-ground play area is dedicated to protected ball games and team sports.

The school has a steel frame crowned with an arched truss at the fourth-floor level: Macalloy bars support the bridge steels in the lightwell, transferring the loads to the truss overhead and enabling the communal hall to be free of columns. The outer envelope is brick, chosen to be sympathetic to the surrounding London stock-brick buildings, while the curve of the play decks is formed by 1.9-metre (6.2-foot) glass balustrading supported on planar-fixed steel uprights. A tensile roof springs from the steel truss, protecting the lightwell below and creating threshold spaces on the roof play area within which to work.

Opposite Detail of curved front

Right Section

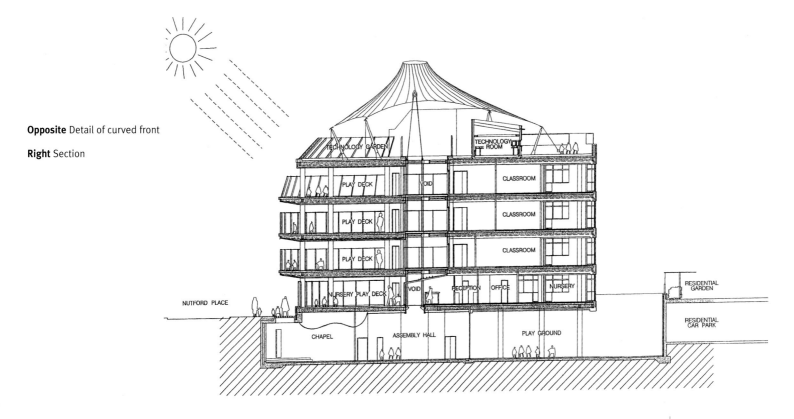

Above School from the street

Right Site plan

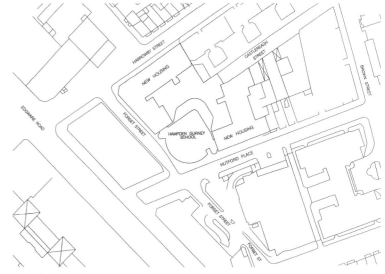

School Builders

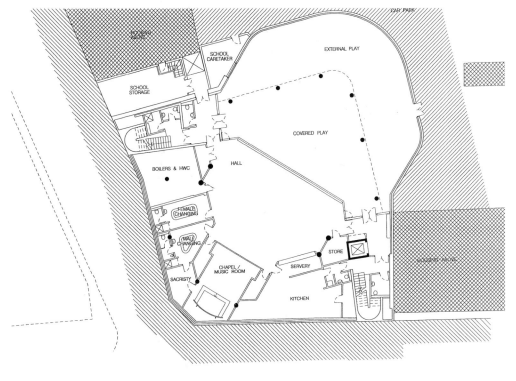

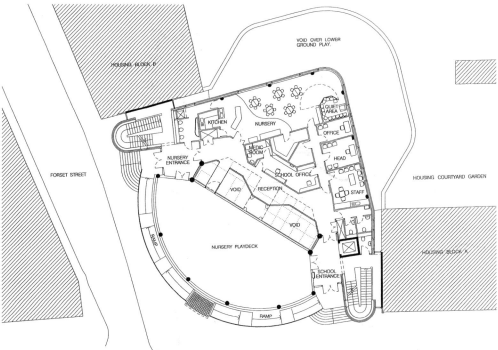

Left Lower ground floor

Below left Ground floor plan

Below right Detail of curved front

External view of curved glazed front, constructed from toughened, laminated glass

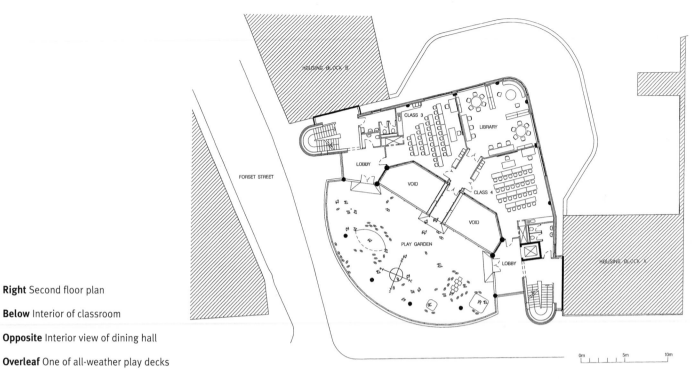

Right Second floor plan

Below Interior of classroom

Opposite Interior view of dining hall

Overleaf One of all-weather play decks

Above West elevation

Right Site plan

RIO DEL NORTE ELEMENTARY SCHOOL

Oxnard, California, US

Rio del Norte Elementary School is located in the City of Oxnard in a new residential neighbourhood. The campus houses 650 children from kindergarten through to elementary, and shares its facilities with the local community.

Construction included infrastructure to support electronic communications and teaching aids, including personal computers, wide-screen closed-circuit televisions, computer networks and VCRs. Classrooms are enhanced with 'smart walls' that integrate electronic and basic support systems.

Classroom clusters are configured so that each building is entered through a formal facade, with the children circulating through a central technical lab to reach their classrooms. Each cluster has an accompanying detached rest-room building available all hours for public use.

Energy-conserving design features provide natural light and ventilation throughout the building; pyramid skylights illuminate the classrooms, operable windows are glazed with high-performance glass, while ceiling fans are used to circulate air to increase comfort and alleviate the need for air conditioning.

The site draws from the axis of the southwest courtyard, which is bright and colourful, to create a stimulating environment for learning. Activity zones provide a variety of indoor and outdoor learning spaces from the large focal point of the amphitheatre to the community-gathering plaza and other spaces. The buildings form a secure environment for the children and teachers without the need for a fence.

Front entrance

Below Floor plan
1 Multi-purpose
2 Administration
3 PTA room
4 Library/LRC
5 Computer lab
6 Kindergarten
7 Classroom
8 Tech lab
9 Restroom kiosk
10 Amphitheatre
11 Courtyard
12 Play area

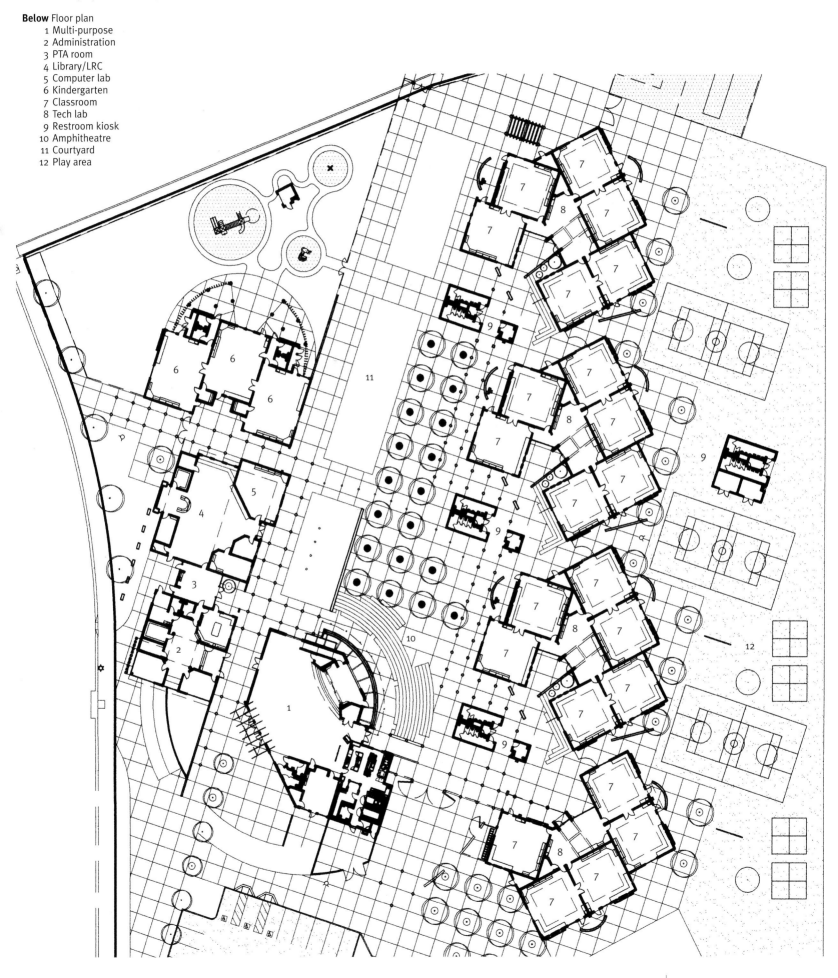

Left Detail of classroom entry as seen through restroom and covered walkway

Right Side entry to kindergarten

Left Interior of pyramid classroom with 'smart walls'

Below Pyramid classroom clusters facing playground

Rio del Norte Elementary School

Multipurpose room, stage and serving kitchen

Kindergarten classroom with 'smart walls'

Above External view of south elevation at night

Opposite Site plan

ST ALOYSIUS JUNIOR SCHOOL

Garnethill, Glasgow, Scotland

In order to strengthen the bond between its upper and lower school and maintain its presence in the city centre, St Aloysius College developed the junior school on the existing college campus. The challenge for Elder and Cannon Architects was to design an effective school within the tight constraints of a site restricted by the shallow urban grid and the context of the cityscape (St Aloysius is located next to Charles Rennie Mackintosh's Glasgow School of Art).

The junior school is a similar scale to the neighbouring buildings, but has contemporary components in line with the vertical emphasis of the tenement. The client wanted a light and airy building within the framework of traditional classrooms, and recognised the contribution that large windows could make in improving the environment of the classrooms. The five-storey south elevation was designed to encourage the maximum amount of air and light into the classes yet layered to give shade and privacy. It uses solar shading among a chequerboard of recessed and projected windows. To the rear, the building steps down three storeys, respecting the scale and amenity of the adjacent back courts. The rear lane is used as a controlled drop-off point for parents, and a newly established side lane connects the main college to the playing fields.

The school is organised vertically. Classrooms are raised above the ground floor to maximise security and privacy, and are organised around a triple-height central stairwell/atrium creating a light and airy orientation space; this has the advantage both of bringing natural light deep into the plan, limiting the requirements for artificial lighting throughout the building, while creating a passive stack effect, reducing the need for forced ventilation.

Each south-facing class has a full -height window wall, divided into two bays. One has fixed blinds to maximise light but reduce glare and filter the view to limit distractions. In the other, computer-controlled enamelled glass louvres provide solar shading, but offer clearer views to the outside while maintaining privacy, allowing the patio doors behind to open for increased ventilation in summer.

Awards
RIBA Award, Civic Trust Award (Commendation), Scottish Design Awards (Runner-Up Best Public Building), Royal Scottish Academy (Art Club Prize), Glasgow Institute of Architects Award.

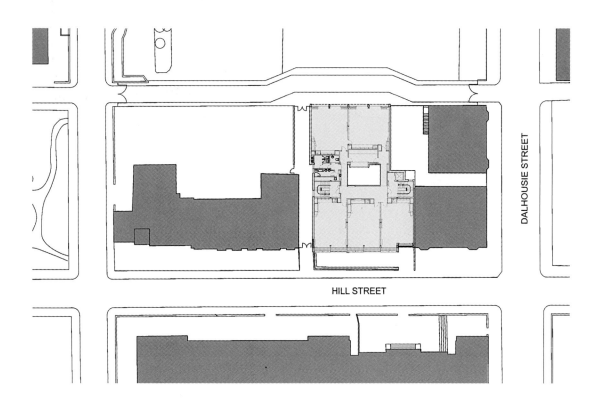

HILL STREET

DALHOUSIE STREET

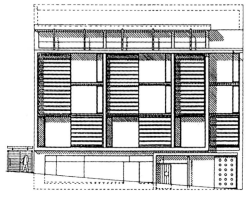

Above left Sketch

Above right Detail of south elevation

Right View of school from the street

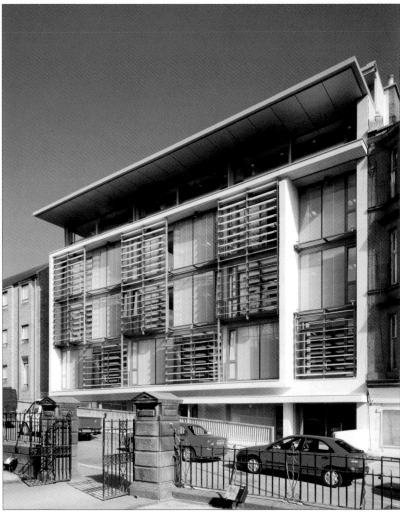

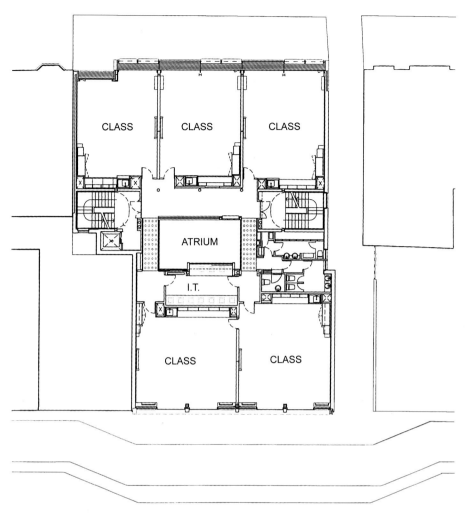

CLASS   CLASS   CLASS

ATRIUM

I.T.

CLASS   CLASS

Left First floor plan

Below Interior view of entrance

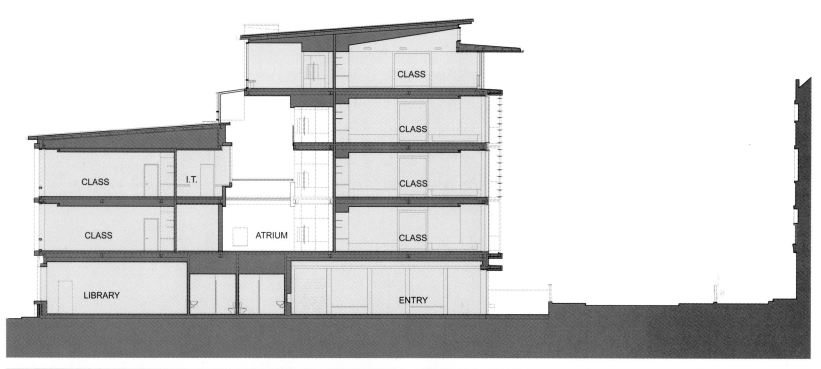

Opposite Detail of atrium looking up

Top Section

Bottom left Interior of classroom

Bottom right Detail of triple height atrium

St Aloysius Junior School

Top Side view of school

Bottom Sections

QUEENS INCLOSURE PRIMARY SCHOOL

Hampshire, England

Queens Inclosure Primary School was built using a very simple plan. At the entrance to the site is a rectangular open space; adjoining and forming the T-shape of the plan is the long rectangular school building, with a stunning backdrop of trees – the Queens Inclosure. It is an open, transparent, light solution that forges a relationship between the grand open landscape outside with light and shade inside.

The school is organised around a central spine that runs the length of the school and is lit overhead by a shallow glazed barrel vault. Teaching spaces, shared areas and specialist facilities are grouped into semi open-plan served areas, while offices, WCs, the hall, music room and main entrance reception are cellular and grouped together. Children can learn by doing and learn by watching in this way.

The building is located on the northern boundary of the Queens Inclosure. A perimeter development between dense woodland to the north and open meadows to the south has established facilities to bridge the gap. The long sides of the main building are fully glazed and protected from the sun by horizontal louvres. The glazed walls of the classrooms face north, into the woods, so there is less sun yet green views; sunlight is reflected into these rooms by this system of louvres supported on steel frames. On the south (where there are communal spaces, such as the hall), a similar canopy has been built to protect the glass walls from over-insulation.

The roof is made up of three parallel barrel vaults that run the length of the rectangle. Each of the two outer vaults has a span of 10 metres (33 feet) and is made of high-tensile corrugated aluminium.

The internal layout is light and airy, due to the natural light brought into the building by the translucent vault. Colours are as industrial as the outer materials – grey and white – but the red furniture adds warmth and colour.

Wide view of school

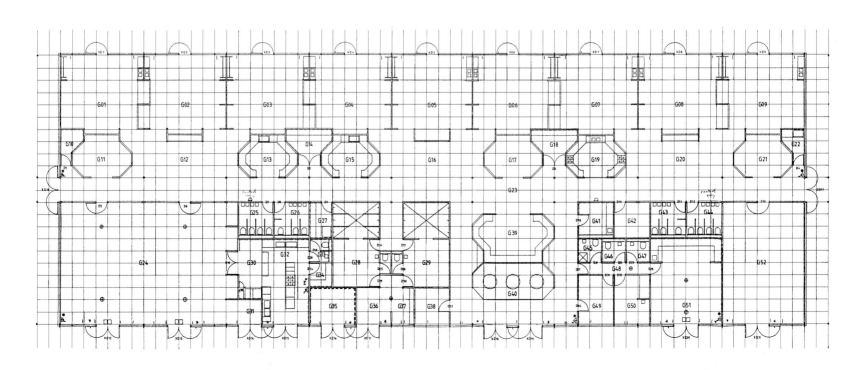

Opposite top left Interior view of central spine lit by a glazed barrel vault

Opposite top right Interior of spine from the outside

Opposite bottom Ground floor plan

Left Interior of classroom

Below left Long side of school shaded by louvres

Below right Corner of school, long side, showing louvres

Top Wide view of school showing one-in-two slope

Centre East elevation

Bottom left Detail of end of classroom wing with storage areas

Bottom right Detail of one end of classroom wing

STAKES HILL INFANT SCHOOL

Hampshire, England

Stakes Hill Infant school was built in the grounds of an existing junior school, on a north-facing site, formerly the gardens of a large house. The junior school takes up the flatter part of the site and the new infant school the more steeply sloping section.

The north–south axis of the new school, the steep slope and the geometry of the site were the key elements in defining the design. The main entrance was set at the lower-floor level of the existing junior school, ensuring a same-level connection between the two. The building has two distinct structural and material systems – load-bearing masonry walls and flat grass-covered roofs built into cuttings in the hillside, and a predominantly timber structure with sloping roofs and timber decks extending out of the building, increasingly above ground level as the site slopes away.

Each classroom has a different outlook – some to the junior school, some to the landscape, some to the coppice to the north – and external play courts surround the classrooms following the fall of the land and separated by landscape strips.

The three wings of classrooms are arranged in two groups of three, and one of four, separated by shared areas with glazed roofs. All classrooms have timber decks used as class entrances and offering external teaching areas. Constructed largely from timber, these classrooms also ensure good levels of natural daylight and ventilation. The classroom wings are constructed largely from timber, with post and beam external walls, curved laminated timber beams and a laminated timber 'tree' structure supporting the upper edge of the three roofs. The 'tree' structure of the roof support, consisting of staggered circular solid timber columns with diagonal struts supporting the roof beam, creates a space filled with light and shadows.

The other main spaces – the school hall, staff offices, music room and kitchen – are housed within a group of linked brick boxes. These spaces have roof levels relating to the scale of the internal spaces and interlock with the ends of the classroom wings.

The school relies on high levels of insulation and consistent insulation constructions together with good levels of natural daylight and natural cross-ventilation. Materials were chosen to reduce embodied energy content and came from sustainable sources (European softwoods, managed hardwoods and managed cedar shingle roofing). The design of the walls for the 'quiet' spaces is based on a 'warm' construction principle that has a higher than normal level of thermal performance.

Dense planting around the perimeter of the building hides the one-in-two slope, which starts flat and rises to 3.5 metres (11 feet) high at the north end. Advantage has been taken of the height at this section to provide storage for outside play and sports equipment.

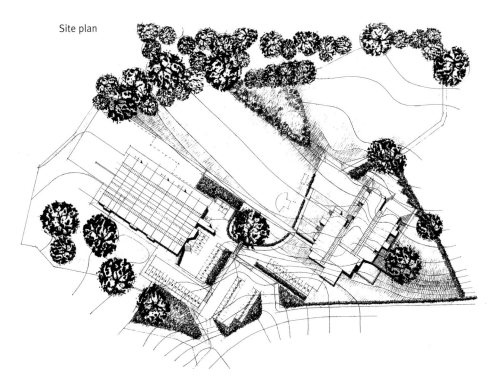

Site plan

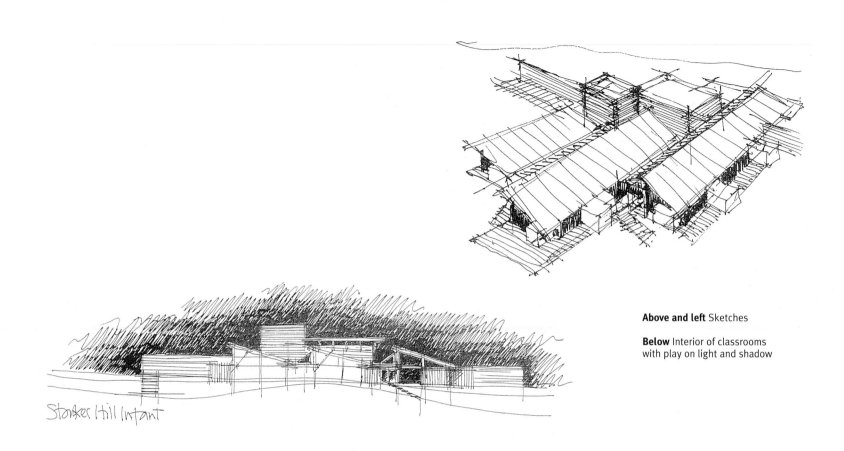

Above and left Sketches

Below Interior of classrooms
with play on light and shadow

Stonker Hill Infant

School Builders

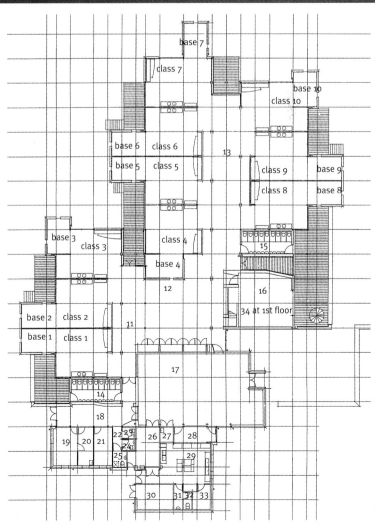

Top left Interior of classrooms showing natural daylight

Top right Interior showing curved ply ceiling

Bottom left Detail of ceiling and windows

Bottom right General layout plan

class 1-10	general class area	23, 24 staff WC
base 1-10	class bases	25 disabled WC &shower
11, 13	shared area	26 caretaker
12	library & resources	27 cleaners store
14, 15	toilets	28 servery/chair store
16	music and drama	29 kitchen
17	school hall	30 plant room
18	reception	31 kitchen cloaks
19	school office	32 kitchen WC
20	medical inspection	33 dry food store
21	head teacher	34 staff room
22	corridor	

WHITELEY PRIMARY SCHOOL

Hampshire, England

The Whiteley site is set in woodland but with a massive water main running diagonally across it. The aim was to use a people-based approach to design, with attention to sustainability, energy and access issues. With a limited budget and a relatively small site for the number of children, the curved design has resulted in a building promoting awareness of its natural surrounds.

The classroom spaces, running west to east, are shaded from summer sun by large overhangs. The sweeping pitched roof has large areas of patent double glazing providing high levels of north light and ventilation. The the infant and junior schools are either side of the central shared areas. For added security, administration and staff facilities flank the entrance. To the north are two blocks with kitchen/hall and community facilities. A terrace outside the classes is retained by a planted bank and provides access down to the main playground. Across the stream, some woodland was cleared for a games pitch.

Materials used were sustainable and durable: brick, timber, shingle roofs and aluminium glazing systems. High standards of wall and roof insulation in addition to the natural lighting of the spaces help to keep electricity bills down.

The design of the overall school is ongoing, with the community facilities still being developed. Contact is maintained with the school to help development of the whole school environment. The design and use of the building is also used for teaching about sustainability. The design team claim that making children and teachers aware of energy and pollution issues has helped create a culture where over 80 per cent of children now cycle or walk to school, and many also check whether lights are left on when not necessary. Providing an environment like Whiteley has, they claim, had an enormous effect on the development, behaviour and well-being of the pupils.

Opposite top Whiteley school from the south

Opposite bottom All classes open on to raised terraces

Below Model of Whiteley

Top left Roof detail at infant school

Top right Detail of daylighting and vents

Right Site plan

Proposed junior classroom

Existing school

School Builders

Left Roof glazing detail of hall

Bottom left Interior of hall

Bottom right Detail of windows and vents at junior school

Above Outside deck of classroom looking across bowl

Right Ground floor plan

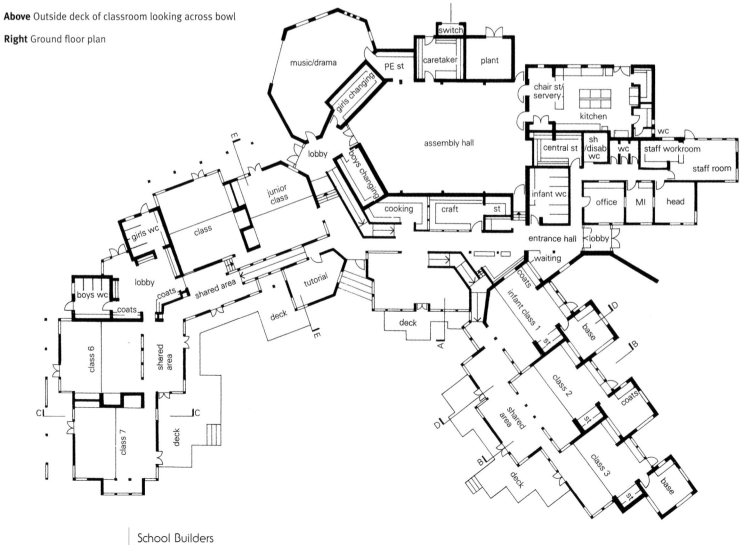

music/drama

switch

PE st

caretaker

plant

chair st/
servery

kitchen

girls changing

wc

assembly hall

central st

sh
/disab
wc

wc

staff workroom

lobby

boys changing

infant wc

staff room

junior
class

office

MI

head

girls wc

class

cooking

craft

st

entrance hall

lobby

waiting

lobby

coats

shared area

tutorial

coats

infant class 1

base

boys wc

coats

deck

deck

class 2

coats

class 6

shared
area

deck

shared
area

class 7

deck

class 3

base

WOODLEA PRIMARY SCHOOL

Hampshire, England

Woodlea Primary School is a unique school-building project. Set in dense woodland the architects had to conceive of a design that would work with the surrounding landscape and manage the steep slope upon which the site lay. The aim was to set the building and recreation areas within this wonderful landscape with the least disturbance possible and in a manner compatible with the safe running of a primary school.

The school is set to the west of the site and follows the existing contours of a natural bowl, although it changes level only twice, totalling just over a metre in difference. The main entrance areas are at the middle level, while ramped circulation leads up to the hall and music/drama areas and then down in the opposite directions to the infant and junior teaching areas. The hard, wet, noisier teaching areas are on the outside of the curve, while the soft, dry, quieter zones focus in on the bowl, opening on to timber decks used for study, play, access and fire escape. Both areas offer maximum flexibility and maximise the use of internal/external relationships.

The inner areas are of timber construction, with suspended carpeted joist and board floors, timber and glass cladding and natural timber ceilings. The tiled floors set on the natural level of the building are terracotta with insets of coloured tiles with different themes designed by the children and executed by a 'guest artist'. External decks are hardwood, and external timber treatment is in eleven 'earth' colours developed by the architects.

Natural lighting is achieved through the use of patent glazing roof-lighting, clerestories and lanterns. Plain-pitched ceilings reflect down daylight and artificial light from uplighters to give even, glare-free lighting.

The siting, layout and sections of the building all take into account the microclimate and passive solar management. The combination of floor, wall and roof insulation, and 90 per cent double glazing, has resulted in very low energy consumption.

'The design and realisation of this school was intended from the outset to bring together many different elements to produce what was hoped could be as near as possible a "total learning environment" – somewhere with as rich a mix as possible in which to educate young children. We were lucky to be given a wonderful site, which will be used to embrace and extend "learning through landscape"' (Hampshire County Council Architects project document).

Awards
Education Award (1991/92), Regional and National RIBA Award (1993), Building of the Year (1993), BBC Design Award for Environment and Architecture (1994).

Infant class and shared area

Left Wide view of school in grounds

Below Site plan
1 Iron Age fort
2 Greenway path
3 Drive and footpath
4 Parking
5 Service
6 Drama garden
7 School garden
8 Main playcourt
9 Pond and dipping deck
10 Playing field path
11 Junior work and play
12 Key tree
13 The bowl
14 Decks
15 The funnel
16 Woods
17 Infant work and play
18 Main entrance
19 Playing field track
20 Playing field
21 Ancient woodland

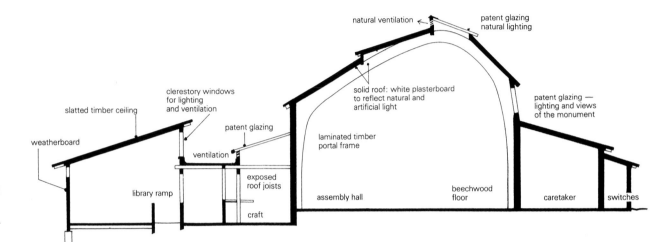

natural ventilation

patent glazing
natural lighting

clerestory windows
for lighting
and ventilation

solid roof: white plasterboard
to reflect natural and
artificial light

slatted timber ceiling

patent glazing —
lighting and views
of the monument

patent glazing

weatherboard

laminated timber
portal frame

ventilation

Right Section

exposed
roof joists

Below left External view of school

library ramp

assembly hall

beechwood
floor

caretaker

switches

Below right Infant class with tiled
floor designed with children

craft

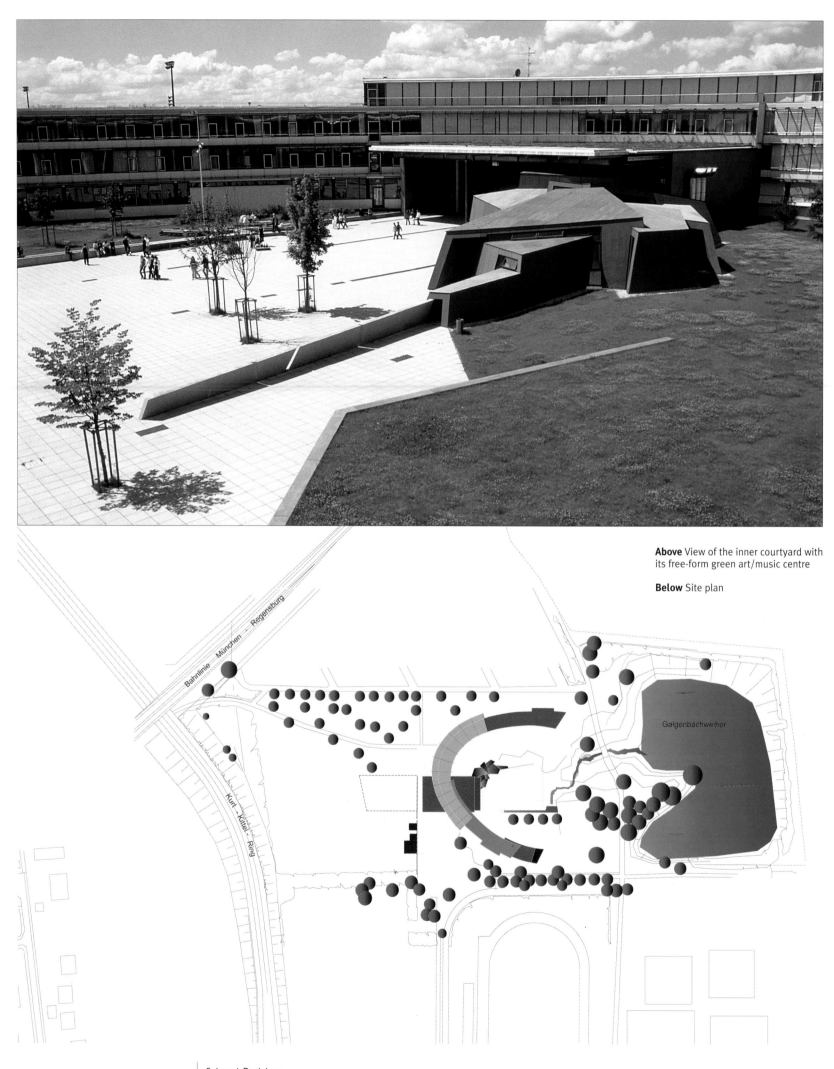

Above View of the inner courtyard with its free-form green art/music centre

Below Site plan

Galgenbachweiher

Bahnlinie München – Regensburg

Kurt - Kittel - Ring

School Builders

OSKAR-MARIA-GRAF-GYMNASIUM
(OSKAR-MARIA-GRAF SECONDARY SCHOOL)

Neufahrn, Germany

Neufahrn required a secondary school for its growing population. The site selected was a level piece of ground on the edge of the town, with no immediate buildings in the vicinity. However, the land itself is surrounded on three sides by noise: a railway line, a ring road and a sports ground. In the east, on the quiet side, there is an old flooded gravel pit that has been converted into a bathing lake; this is the only point of interest across the flat landscape.

Prior to the Neufahrn project, Hein Goldstein had designed a primary school in Pfaffenhofen, and used this as the model to stimulate the new design. In addition, he considered the local context and incorporated contrasting mixtures of building styles used in the town.

Responding to the site, the school building curves away from the sources of noise and embraces the lake on the inner curve. This gesture in the external form carries through to the internal organisation: all classrooms are located on the 'softer' inner side of the curve, and on the 'hard' outer side are corridors and rooms or areas that are less sensitive to noise, for example WCs, storerooms and stairs.

The school is 'encased' in a curved metal sheath, with concrete walls stained in shades of yellow and orange to bring some life to the cold industrial materials. By contrast, the inner courtyard is open-plan and clear. The classrooms are set on four levels on side wings curving out from the central section. The first-floor gallery runs through the hallway, acting as a balcony.

The expressive green structure in the inner courtyard also grew out of the belief that form and content should be adapted to each other. This part of the building contains the school's art facilities, along with the music rooms and the stage. In formal terms, the free shape of the body represents a counterpoint to the exact and strictly geometric curved shape of the main building. On the inside, the many-cornered rooms, with their sloping walls and ceilings, provide a special atmosphere conducive to making music and play-acting.

'The basic preoccupation underlying all formal and architectural considerations during the whole of the planning phase was the effect the finished building would have on the mood and mentality of its users. I am convinced that buildings have a strong influence on the people who live in them. Although the people are usually unaware of this effect, it is very real. All formal decisions were made with this in mind. If our building can help to make the Neufahrn pupils open, free and responsible people, our efforts will be well rewarded,' says Hein Goldstein.

Front detail of staircase on outer curve

Opposite top left Detail of wing of inner curve

Opposite top right Detail of staircase on outer curve

Opposite bottom left Interior of first floor walkway
overlooking hall

Opposite bottom right Interior detail of art/music centre

Top Interior of walkway overlooking courtyard

Bottom Interior detail of art/music centre

Oskar-Maria-Graf-Gymnasium

Opposite top Entrance to the school

Opposite bottom The school facing in on the lake

Left Example of the yellow/orange shaded concrete on the outer walls

Below Students playing music in the music centre

Top Gardens and classrooms at night

Centre North elevation

Bottom South elevation

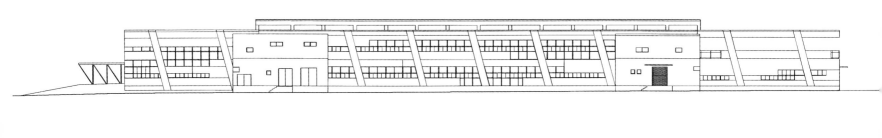

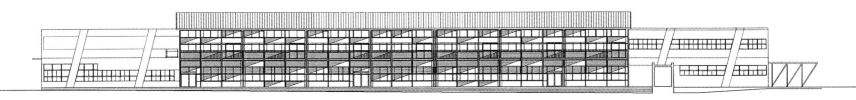

Itsuko Hasegawa

KAIHO ELEMENTARY SCHOOL

Himi, Japan

The population of Himi is spread over a wide area, and its educational districts are also large. The local people take education extremely seriously and maintain ties with their schools long after leaving. The design of Kaiho Elementary School attempted to take this into consideration.

The design reflects the environmental sensibilities of its coastal location, drawing on ocean imagery as a source. The architecture was perceived as part of an overall landscape design rather than the landscape design following on from the architecture (as is more typical).

The long north wing, wave-like in form, consists of classrooms. The central wing houses special educational facilities and communal areas; the south wing houses the gymnasium. All rooms in the wings have moveable partitions and open to the exterior. The grounds are characterised by landscaped hills, a stream and an amphitheatre. The roof gardens are designed to be used as science rooms, reading zones, assembly points and lunch areas.

Architect Itsuko Hasegawa says: 'We believe that this is a new kind of landscape architecture that could be termed "architecture as topography"; it provides the entire community with a "garden school". It is hoped that the pupils will use the school to its full creative potential, respecting the spirit of the local culture while at the same time acting as true representatives for the global information network that characterises today's society.'

Wide view of school

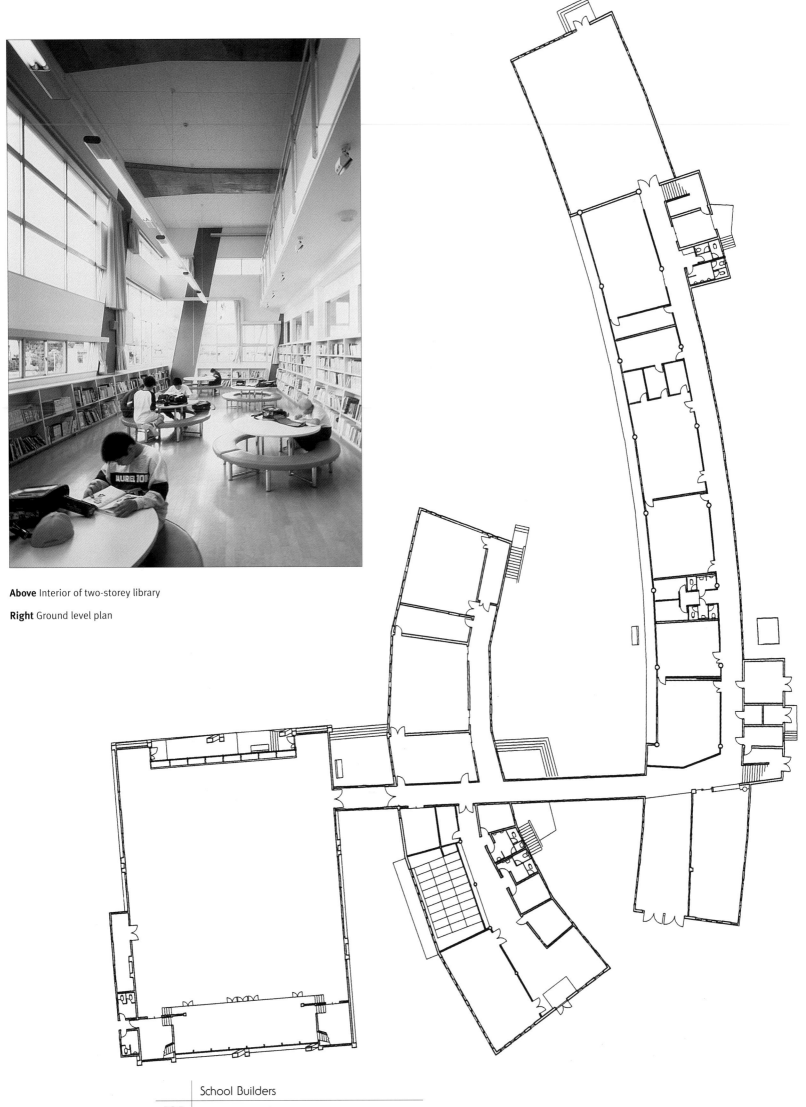

Above Interior of two-storey library

Right Ground level plan

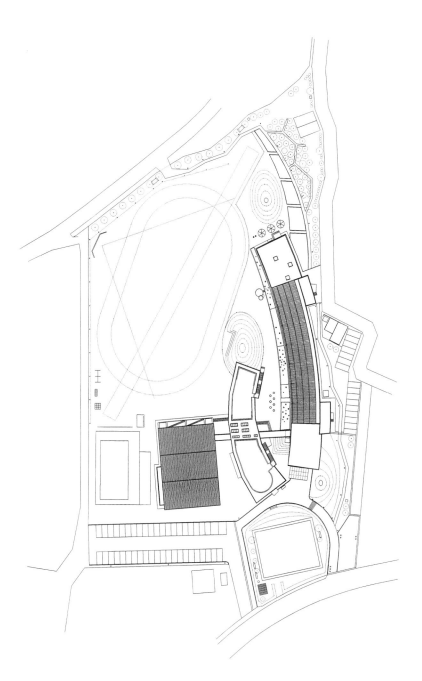

Above left Site plan

Right Long wave-like classroom wing

Bottom Detail of classroom wing

Kaiho Elementary School

LYCÉE FRANÇAIS DE SINGAPOUR
(INTERNATIONAL FRENCH SCHOOL OF SINGAPORE)

Singapore

A school is designed to be a place of passage, a place where living happens. The variety of spaces, their volumes and their styles, makes each route or journey a unique experience. The Grand Lycée is to be a marvellous place for living, anchored in French culture and opening to the twenty-first century

(Annick Bouvier-Feuillade, Principal, Lycée Français de Singapour)

The new Lycée Français in Singapore aims to capture the aspirations of the French community living in Singapore. The major building elements, which take advantage of a north–south orientation, are designed as a noise barrier along the entire frontage of the site, giving the school an impressive roof line with much dignity and character.

The Lycée comprises three schools: a kindergarten, primary and secondary school. It integrates the various educational facilities with common amenities like outdoor play courts, gymnasiums, a theatre, swimming pool and sports track and field. The spaces for each school are distinct and expansive. The school 'floats' above the vehicular circulation route. The bus bay, under the main gymnasium, is designed like a grand arrival space, or bus terminal; fronted by the canteen it opens up internally onto a central courtyard and play space framed by the distinct buildings around it. Each school has a distinct 'precinct' and entry foyer along the main facade, symbolised by each distinct roof made from perforated steel and glass towers, or using a curved perforated metal screen designed to be an abstracted flag in motion.

The priority of the design, according to the architects, is the order of buildings, providing clearly defined public as well as living and work areas for each age group. The materials of the facade and the way they are used help to signal this identity of the buildings: the low kindergarten buildings are timber clad; the medium-sized primary school building is in brick; and the larger secondary school buildings are in steel, compressed fibre cement cladding and glass, with a sweeping metallic roof. The changes children experience as they grow older are translated stylistically by a progression from the use of more traditional types of materials to the contemporary.

Buildability was considered at the outset of the architectural design and detailing, and the logic of assembly informed the composition of the facade. The structural floor slabs are post-tensioned to achieve wide efficient spans. The facade comprises infill panels of 'dry' or prefabricated elements, namely perforated steel sheets, glass and compressed fibre cement boards.

The roof collects rainwater for the sports field and comprises lightweight composite metal panels and aluminium fascia panels. It is tapered in section, elevation and plan, thus achieving a dynamic unified form.

Awards
Building and Construction Authority Best Buildable Design Awards (2001), Singapore Institute of Architects Best Architectural Design Awards (2001), Singapore Institute of Architects Facade Design Excellence Awards – Silver Award (2001).

Opposite top View from the street

Opposite bottom Different types of building clusters signify the different schools

Below Zoning plan showing spatial progression

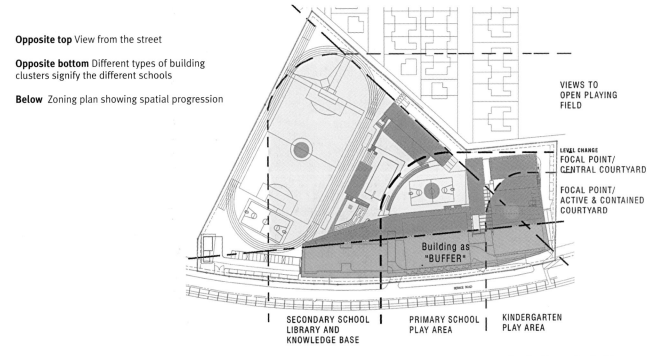

VIEWS TO
OPEN PLAYING
FIELD

LEVEL CHANGE
FOCAL POINT/
CENTRAL COURTYARD

FOCAL POINT/
ACTIVE & CONTAINED
COURTYARD

Building as
"BUFFER"

SERVICE ROAD

SECONDARY SCHOOL
LIBRARY AND
KNOWLEDGE BASE

PRIMARY SCHOOL
PLAY AREA

KINDERGARTEN
PLAY AREA

Lycée Français de Singapour

Above Kindergarten and playground

Below Elevation

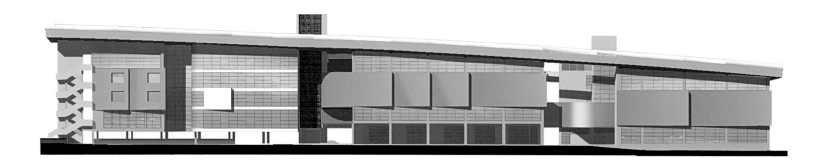

School Builders

Above Facade of primary school

Right Primary school and playground

Above left Secondary school

Above right Detail of outside stairs

Below left Ground floor plan

Below right First floor plan

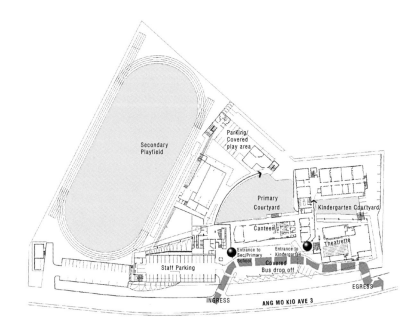

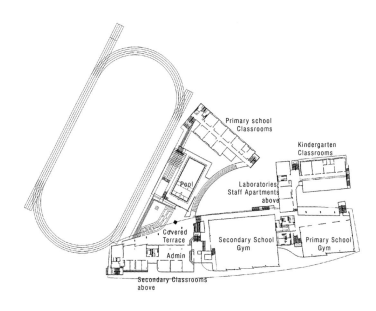

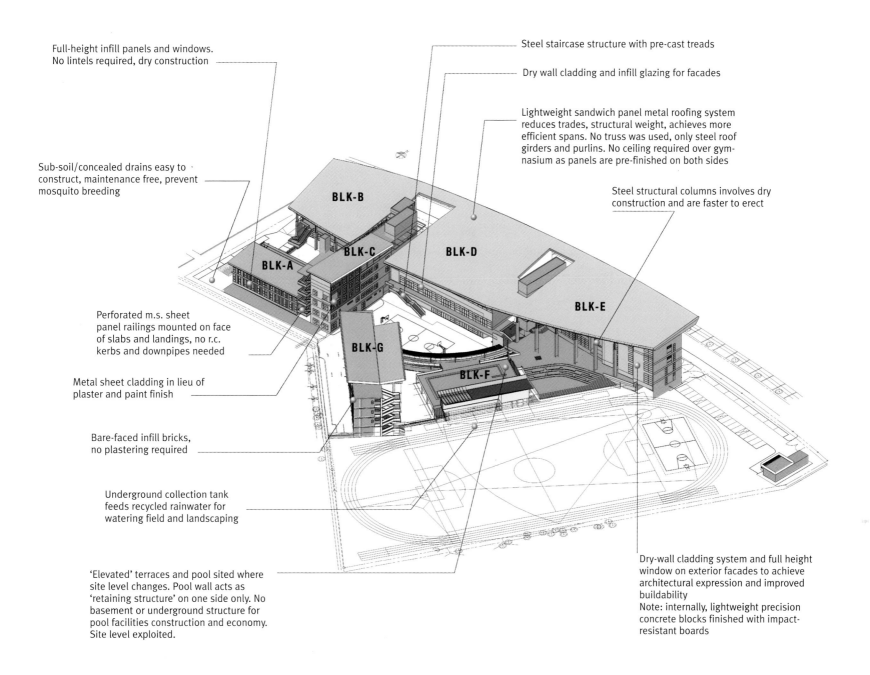

Full-height infill panels and windows. No lintels required, dry construction

Sub-soil/concealed drains easy to construct, maintenance free, prevent mosquito breeding

Perforated m.s. sheet panel railings mounted on face of slabs and landings, no r.c. kerbs and downpipes needed

Metal sheet cladding in lieu of plaster and paint finish

Bare-faced infill bricks, no plastering required

Underground collection tank feeds recycled rainwater for watering field and landscaping

'Elevated' terraces and pool sited where site level changes. Pool wall acts as 'retaining structure' on one side only. No basement or underground structure for pool facilities construction and economy. Site level exploited.

Steel staircase structure with pre-cast treads

Dry wall cladding and infill glazing for facades

Lightweight sandwich panel metal roofing system reduces trades, structural weight, achieves more efficient spans. No truss was used, only steel roof girders and purlins. No ceiling required over gymnasium as panels are pre-finished on both sides

Steel structural columns involves dry construction and are faster to erect

Dry-wall cladding system and full height window on exterior facades to achieve architectural expression and improved buildability
Note: internally, lightweight precision concrete blocks finished with impact-resistant boards

BLK-A
BLK-B
BLK-C
BLK-D
BLK-E
BLK-F
BLK-G

Above Material plan
BLK-A Kindergarten with play areas on 2 levels
BLK-B Primary School /Gymnasium
BLK-C Laboratories/Staff apartments
BLK-D Secondary School/Gymnasium/Canteen
BLK-E Administration Centre/Secondary School
BLK-F Pool & Sports Arena
BLK-G Primary School Block/covered play area

Right Classrooms from the outside

Lycée Français de Singapour

View of outer wall of gym with shaped windows, and glazed staircase that traverses the three levels

TRINITY SCHOOL

Atlanta, Georgia, US

Trinity School is a private elementary school with 500 pupils from pre-kindergarten through to sixth grade. Architects Lord, Aeck & Sargent were commissioned to design a major renovation and expansion on a difficult site that provided new playground areas, an extended library and spaces for art, music, media studies and other enriching spaces previously unavailable at the school.

Designed as a collection of playground pieces, the various elements of the school's design evoke romantic, playful images, creating a fairy-tale environment that makes architecture an intriguing part of the children's learning experience.

Trinity School was established thirty years ago. Limited to a two-storey elementary school on a small site, it was later expanded with two additional classroom wings. The 3-hectares (8-acre) site was not only small by elementary school standards, but also included a 12-metre-deep (40-foot-deep) gorge running right through the site, isolating the school from the land opposite. As the school wished to hold on to its established outdoor recreation space, the architects were persuaded to use the 'unusable' gorge for the expansion project.

The new building, wedged in the gorge, totals 1,900 square metres (20,500 square feet), over half the size of the existing school. Almost half of this area is taken up with a gymnasium, the two-storey inner wall of which is buried in the ravine. The roof of the gymnasium doubles up and is used as the foundation for a two-storey library wrapped by an L-shaped play deck.

Adjoining the massive outer wall of the gymnasium is the cylindrical corner tower that plays on a medieval castle theme with its split-face concrete block alternating with the smooth, and glass holes that enliven the wall with a pattern of twinkling dots. The scale of the windows and building of the castle wall and tower are made even more ambiguous by the placement of three geometric-shaped oversized windows: a triangle for the tower, a diamond for the gym, and a circle straddling the floors of the upper building.

The gorge may be traversed via a fire-engine red bridge from the castle wall back to the land; and the tower hosts an outdoor spiralling staircase that reaches the floor of the gorge, leading to a small amphitheatre. The gorge itself also houses various nature trails and other outdoor educational activities.

Inside, a staircase from the upper deck of the gymnasium building traverses a glazed passage across the three levels, enlivened by the use of vibrant primary colours.

Awards
National American Institute of Architects (AIA) Award (1990), Award for Design Excellence, Georgia Association AIA (1988), Award for Design Excellence, South Atlantic Regional Conference AIA (1987).

Original school buildings

Above Columns at night

Below Upper level plan

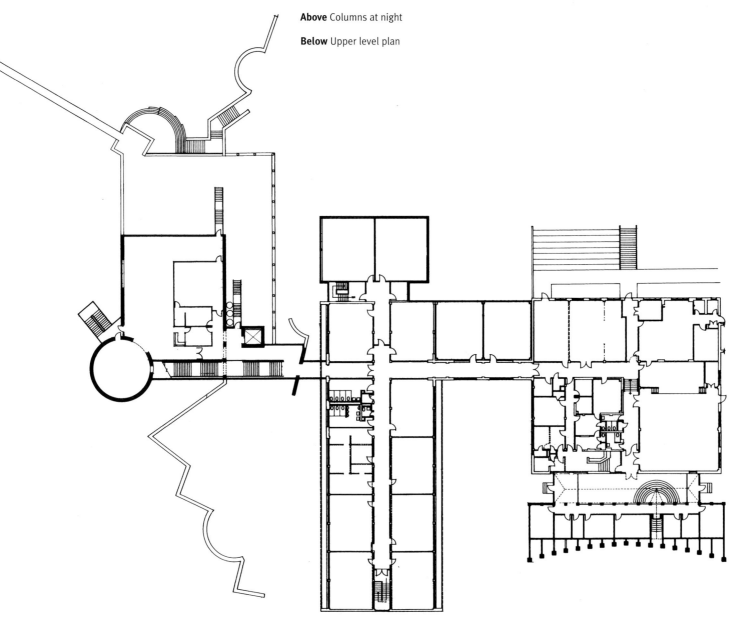

Above View of tower and gym wall at night

Below Axonometric of proposed buildings

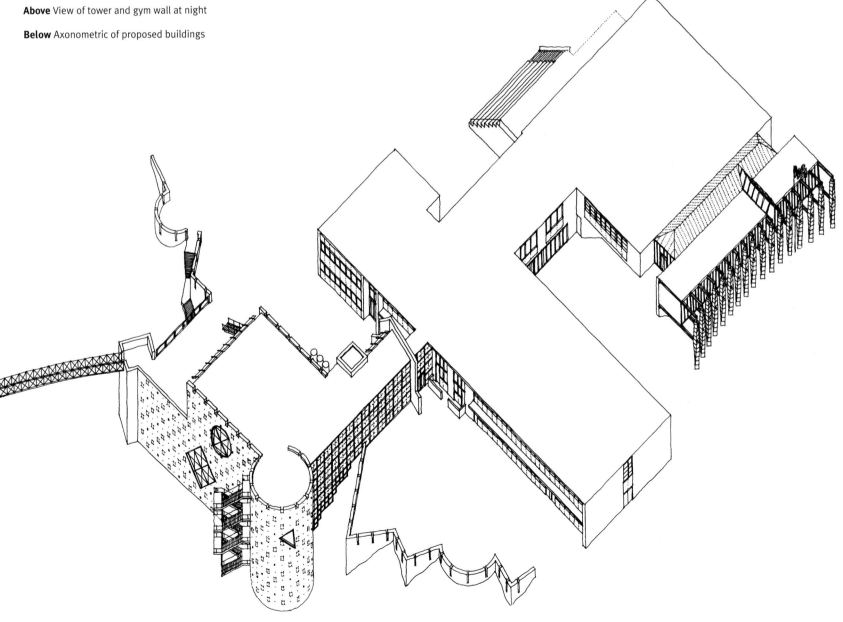

Trinity School

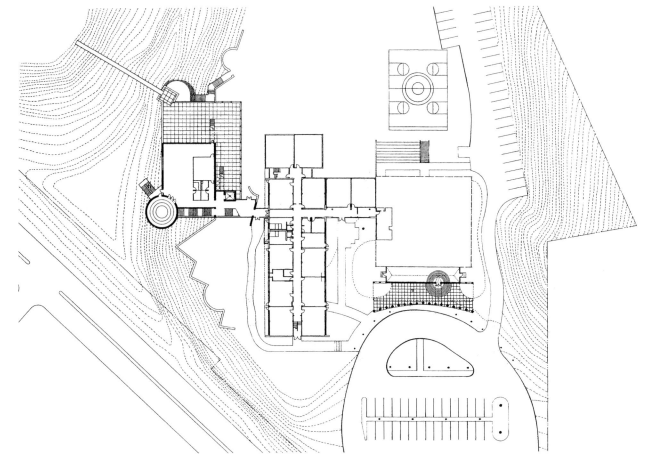

Trinity School

STRAWBERRY VALE ELEMENTARY SCHOOL

British Columbia, Canada

Strawberry Vale Elementary School was built adjacent to the site of an existing single-room schoolhouse that was demolished and relocated elsewhere on the site to be used as a pre-school facility. The site slopes gently from west to east, and south to north by approximately 3 metres (10 feet).

The school is set in a suburban neighbourhood of single-family dwellings with intervals of small-scale agricultural plots and natural wetlands. On the south edge of the school is a park with mature Garry oaks and a number of large rock outcroppings.

There is a strong relationship to nature in the design of the school: for example, classrooms are oriented toward the south to optimise natural lighting within the interior as well as to maximise visual connection to the nearby Rosedale Park. Furthermore, all classrooms are located on-grade, providing direct access to the out-of-doors. This not only maintains a scale consistent with the neighbourhood, but also establishes a positive reciprocity in the definition of park and schoolyard.

To locate classrooms in this way, and keep the length of the school within the limits of the site, classrooms are grouped into pods of four. In so doing a series of 'common' spaces, both interior and exterior, is created. In addition, a variety of moveable carts for art, science and cooking can be 'plugged-in' to these common areas. A meandering circulation spine provides access to each pod and the remaining components of the building programme, such as the library, administration, gymnasium and other support facilities.

Wood is both the most readily accessible and renewable construction material available in British Columbia, and was therefore selected as the principal construction material for the school. Walls and roofs are framed and sheathed with wood; the column and beam members required to support the wooden construction, however, are steel, to avoid the use of 'first-growth' lumber.

Foundations and floors are reinforced concrete, cast-in-place, and located at elevations following the existing grade to minimise site work. The resulting floor plan of the school becomes a representation of the existing grade of the site. Roof slopes, which are extremely shallow to minimise building volume, are clad with aluminium-coated steel.

Generally, materials have been selected to minimise the amount of energy embodied within the building, and potentially toxic materials have been avoided; claddings have therefore been kept to a minimum within the school leaving much of the primary construction of wood, steel and concrete exposed. White-painted gypsum board has been added to complete exterior wall assemblies and where needed on interior wall and ceiling surfaces for luminosity.

Heating and lighting systems are designed to optimise the use of solar energy – heating through simple passive heat gain when sun angles are low, and lighting through the controlled placement of windows, clerestoreys and skylights. The mechanical air-handling system has been left visible in the upper levels of the circulation spine through which it is routed, and is fully accessible to allow easy maintenance. In addition, the natural 'stack effect' resulting from the building cross-section brings fresh air into the classrooms and library via high-level exhaust points, interior transfer grilles and operable windows.

Opposite top External view of school

Opposite bottom Long view of site

Right Interior of gymnasium

Above Side view of school

Below Section

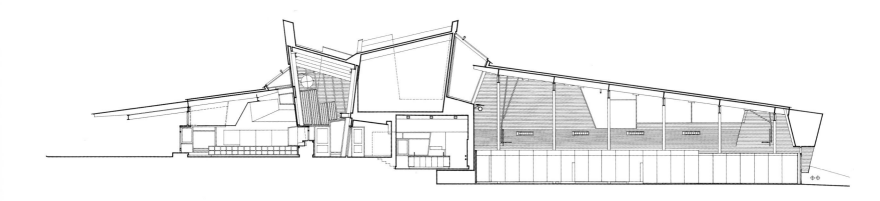

School Builders

Above View from the classroom

Below Section

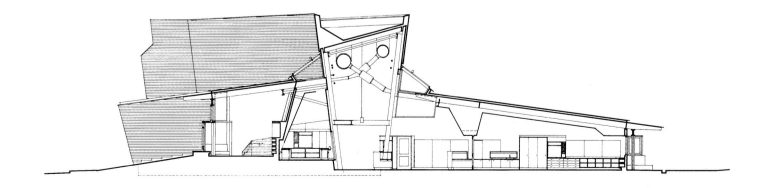

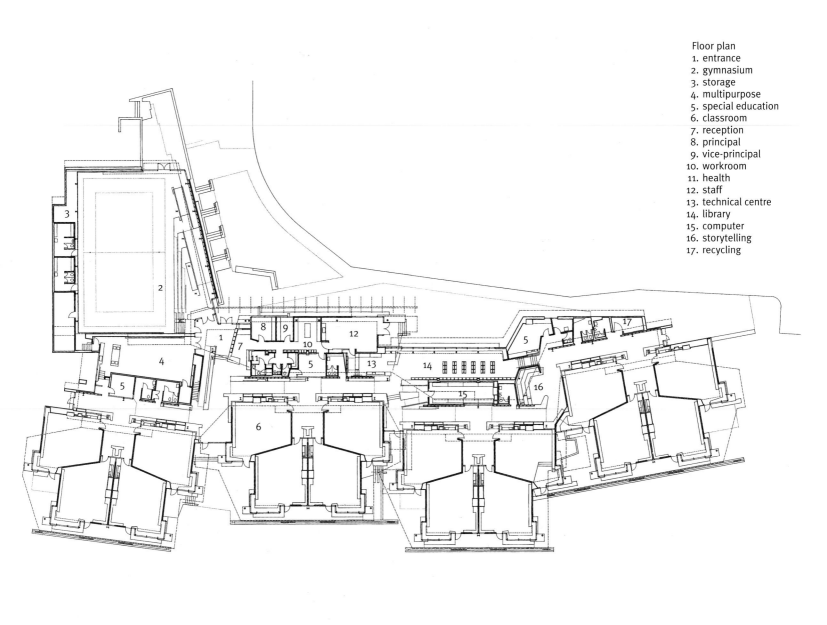

Floor plan
1. entrance
2. gymnasium
3. storage
4. multipurpose
5. special education
6. classroom
7. reception
8. principal
9. vice-principal
10. workroom
11. health
12. staff
13. technical centre
14. library
15. computer
16. storytelling
17. recycling

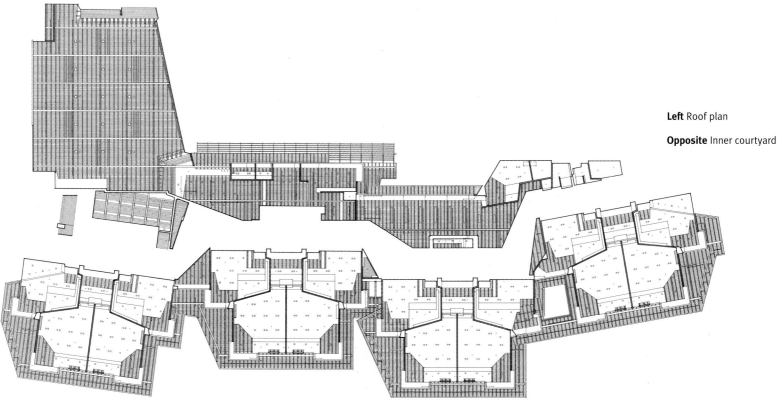

Left Roof plan

Opposite Inner courtyard

Strawberry Vale Elementary School

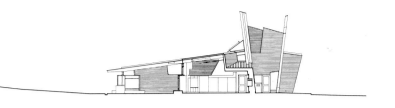

Opposite Interior view of library

Left Sections

Below left Walkways amongst different levels in the interior

Below right Interior details of exposed structures of roof

Strawberry Vale Elementary School

Above View from within courtyard

Opposite Main entrance

DESERT VIEW ELEMENTARY SCHOOL

New Mexico, US

Perkins & Will developed this cool, colourful yet budget-conscious prototype elementary school in the middle of New Mexico's arid desert terrain, serving a very poor district with a mostly immigrant population. Using simple concrete blocks and bar joists, encircled by a low curving rock wall, Desert View Elementary School works out at about $50 per square foot. Inspired by the local small-scale architecture, Perkins & Will created a colourful abstraction of these basic elements while keeping costs down and the desert out (including concrete blocks, corrugated metal, steel posts and glass-fibre panels).

Instead of building one big campus to accommodate all of the expected student population, three identical facilities were repeated about a quarter of a mile apart utilising the readily available land parcels on the outskirts of the community.

The square plan of the buildings is simple with standard-sized classrooms on either side of the larger shared spaces, and halls accessed through open courtyards and plazas, giving a village feeling within the school. The spaces are cooled, despite its desert context, with walkways shaded by translucent fibreglass roofs and canvas awnings. The larger spaces – such as the gymnasium and the auditorium – are to be shared with the local community.

The variety of windows – from the tiny to the entire gable ends – give the building a much larger sense of scale than its relatively modest size would typically evoke. In addition, the colour detail in the concrete bearing walls and the bright paint of the exposed steel structure give a festive elegance to the materials. In addition, the school is encircled by a low rock wall acting as a divide between the irrigated plant areas adjoining the buildings and the surrounding sandy desert.

The evident interplay between light and shade indoors and out in this prototype desert school will be even more defined once the landscaping within the encircling rock wall matures. Despite the interiors being left as they are – concrete blocks, metal roofs and steel structures – the exposed bar joists, painted green, provide a subtle but familiar indigenous touch.

Top View of school from the road

Bottom Detail of canopy awnings used in walkways

Right Site plan

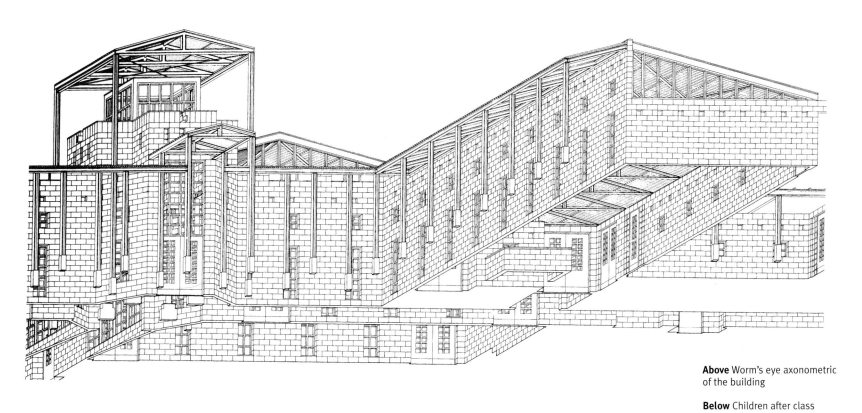

Above Worm's eye axonometric of the building

Below Children after class

Desert View Elementary School

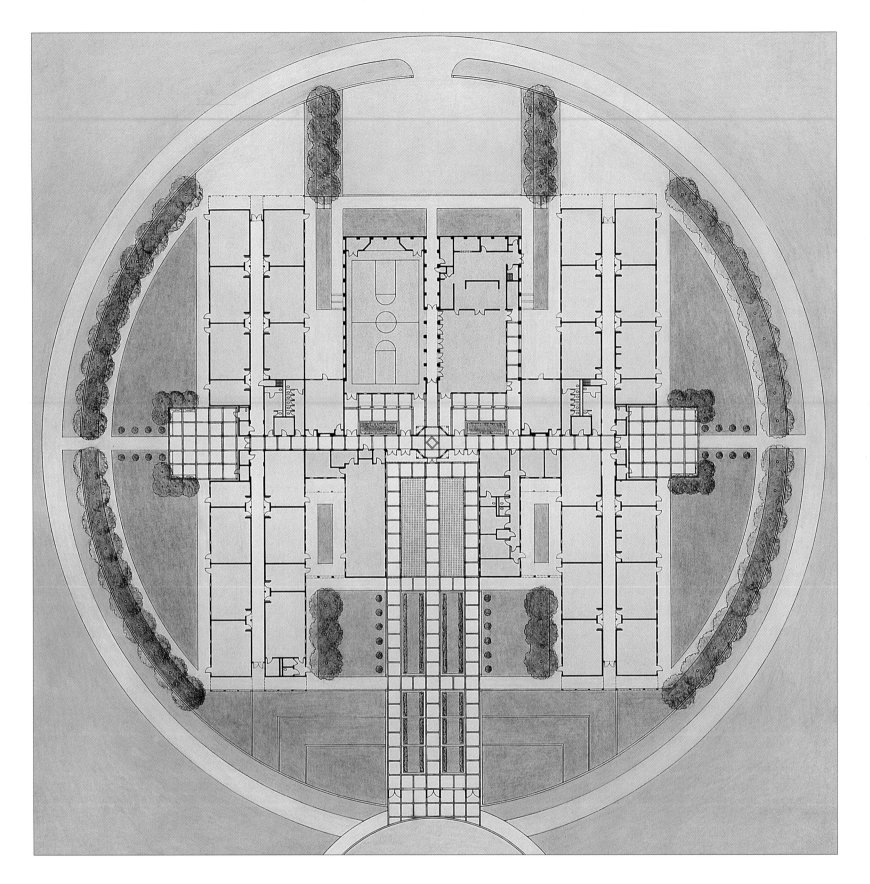

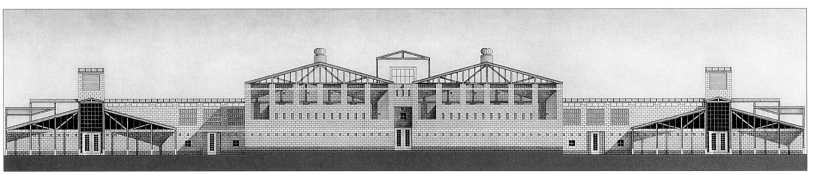

Opposite top Site plan

Opposite bottom Elevation

Above left Detail of tower in main entrance

Above right Detail of fibreglass roofs used in walkways

Opposite Interior of corridor

Above Gadsden Elementary School, Sunland
Park – another of the set of three schools

View of new media centre

NORTH FORT MYERS SCHOOL

North Fort Myers, Florida, US

At North Fort Myers School, Perkins & Will were presented with an existing site that comprised school buildings from the 1950s, 1960s and 1970s with disparate styles of architecture. The architects were asked to utilise what they could, and come up with a fully up-to-date facility, planned so that construction would not interfere with the ongoing operations of the school. This posed logistical and architectural difficulties.

The existing campus did not really have a centre, or central space, for gathering, and the architects' solution to this became a focus in their design strategy. A simple composition that 'would pull everything together again' was selected, its simple geometry basically a bar and a circle.

The new media centre is housed within the circle, cutting the courtyard at an angle. It is a triangular-shaped, sloped-roof building surrounded by a two-storey circular classroom building, and is considered the heart of the school as it houses the library, computer classrooms and radio/television laboratory. The angle of the building not only gives the courtyard a distinctive shape but also ties the new buildings in with the old (an existing building was already set askew on the site). Other renovations include the gymnasium and an old classroom building that have become the new cafeteria and art studios.

The corridors of the classroom building are covered, and public spaces are either courtyards or covered walkways offering protection from the strong Florida sun; though the covered walkways let natural light into the classrooms, they are at the same time shielded from direct sunlight.

Classrooms are conventional in plan and design. However, the environmental studies programme offered by the school has allowed for some interesting details: a preserved wetland area adjacent to the car park and an experimental garden for the exploration of native plants and ecological studies.

The main construction material used is brick, as requested by the client, in beige, buff and terracotta.

Detail from inside circular classroom building

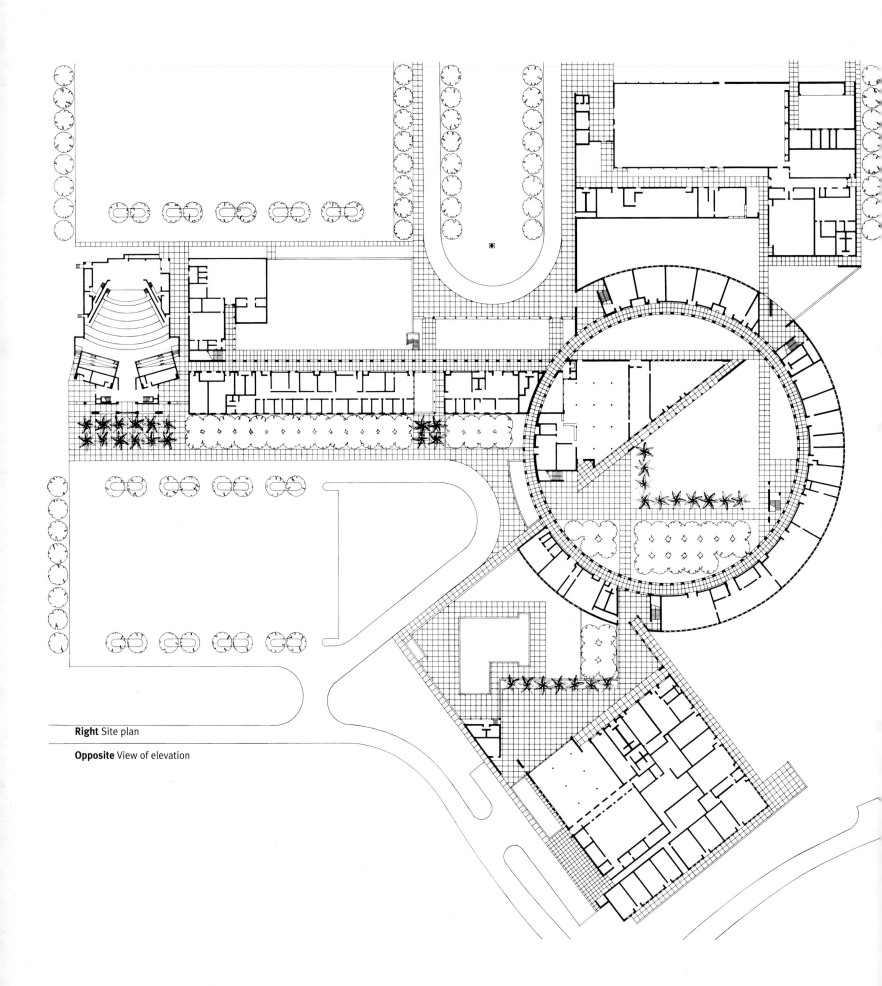

Right Site plan

Opposite View of elevation

New media centre's sloping roof and circular classroom building

Detail of sun-protecting eaves and different brickwork of new media centre

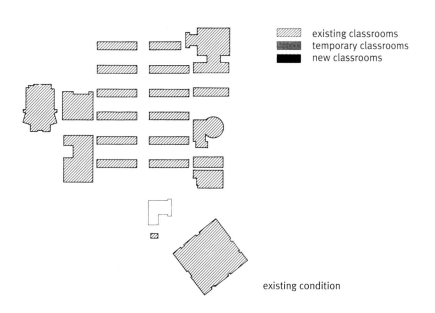

existing classrooms
temporary classrooms
new classrooms

existing condition

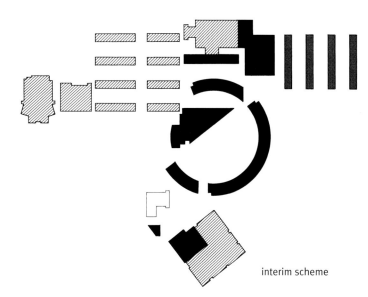

interim scheme

Opposite View from inside circular classroom building

Left Intermediate stages plan

Below View of an entrance

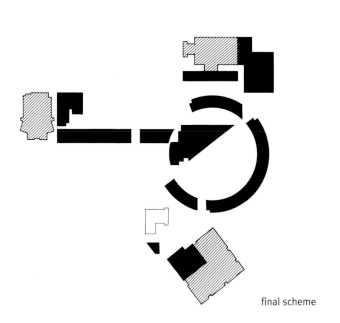

final scheme

North Fort Myers School

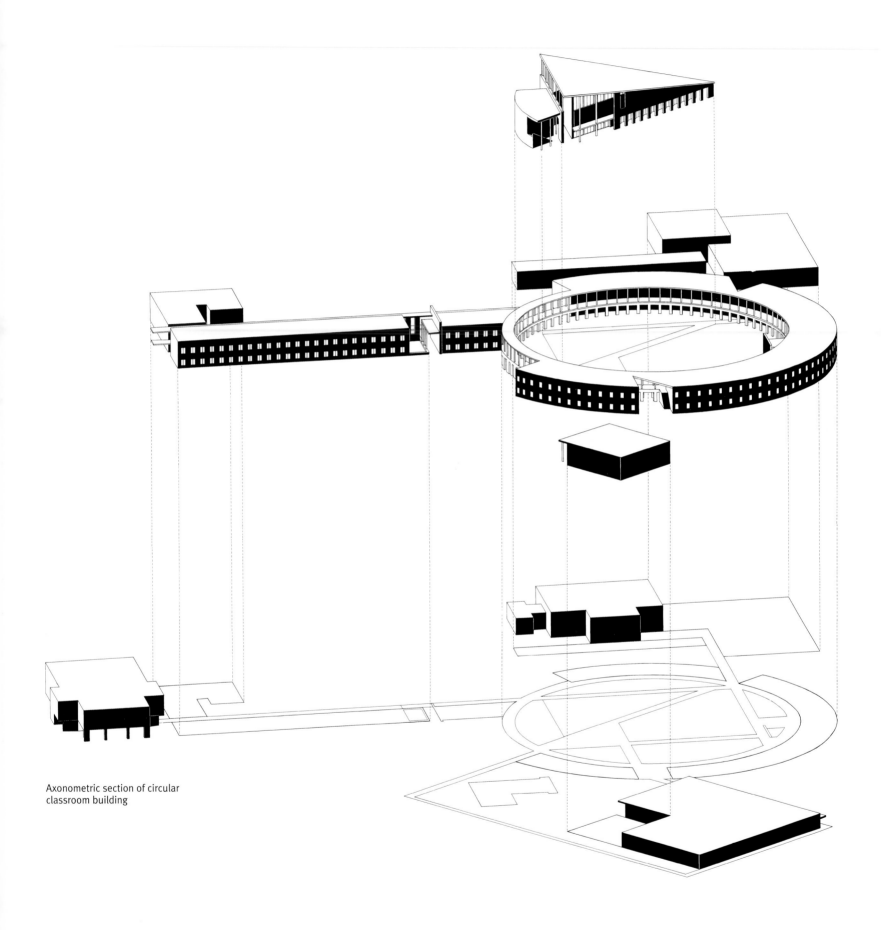

Axonometric section of circular
classroom building

Left Interior of library

Below Ground floor plan

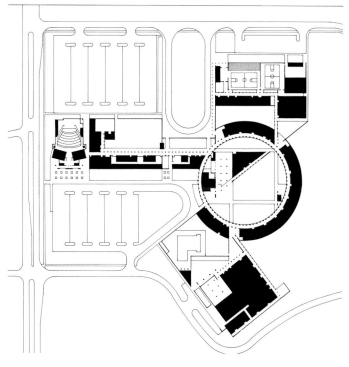

Above Classroom facade

Opposite External view of campus

PERRY COMMUNITY EDUCATION VILLAGE

Unusually set in the flat Midwestern plains, Perry Local School District's new Community Education Village comprises four elements: a school for kindergarten through grade four; a school for grades five through eight; a high school; and a physical education/community fitness centre.

The $95 million project (revenue for which came from a local nuclear power plant) was built in two phases. The first phase consisted of the high school, a hi-tech theatre and a community sports centre. The second phase completed the middle and lower schools, built on the other side of the banks of Red Mill Creek.

The 'education village' was conceived as a way of lowering costs; for example, three schools in one campus could share power output from a centralised plant, use the same gymnasium and theatre, as well as the other facilities. The pupils also benefit from shared access to aspects of the curriculum otherwise restricted to older students. Each school within the village is designed to accommodate 1,500 pupils and fits into a natural clearing. All classrooms enjoy scenic views of the surrounding woodlands. Three tributaries of Red Mill Creek have cut natural ravines on the site, and one ravine serves to separate the lower from the upper grades. The lower and upper facilities are organised around formal courtyards, which are connected by an enclosed walkway bridging the ravine.

The three schools manage to be more or less independent by way of plan. The lower school is off to the north side of the middle school, with a separate pick-up area for children, while the middle and high school are connected merely by a narrow suspension bridge. It was the aim of the architects to make the divisions between the schools as explicit as possible so that the pupils would appreciate the progression from one school to the next. A massive sports complex dominates the southern edge of the site.

An enclosed pedestrian bridge is anchored at each end by twin cafeterias. This central spine continues from the bridge beyond the high-school dining areas to the main theatre, which is occasionally shared by all of the pupils at the same time.

Perkins & Will have tended to use similar forms for buildings of similar functions, which can give the campus a feeling of shared identity. For example, the classrooms in all of the schools are designed as if cut at different places from one length of structure, establishing recognisable typologies.

The architects have taken as source the local industrial buildings that line the major river in the region (the Erie). In addition, there is a slim tower that marks the entrance to the theatre and sports centre, as a counterpoint to the cooling towers of the nuclear plant across the landscape.

The three arts buildings are tipped with fan-like structures with interlocking pitched roofs, offering a covered terrace for activities. The maximum height of the theatre reaches up to 30 metres (98 feet) high and dominates views of the high school. The curving structure to its right is the theatre itself, which flanks the central courtyard of the high school.

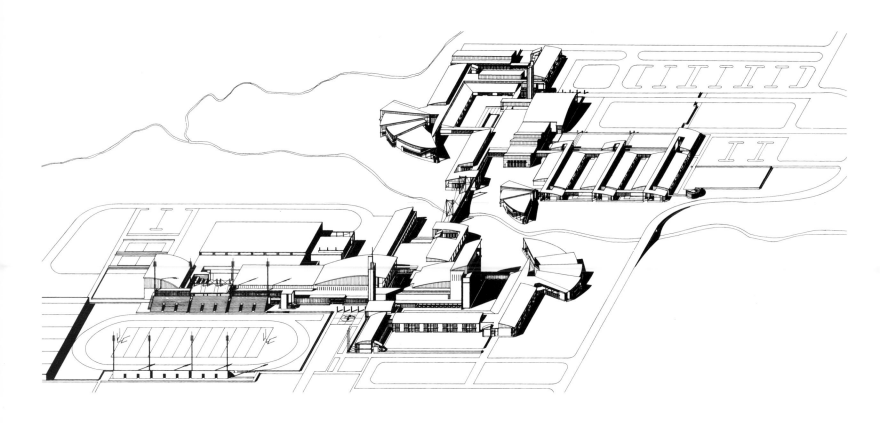

Above Site plan

Opposite top Fan-like tip of one of the arts buildings

Opposite bottom View of classrooms at dusk

Opposite Interior of music complex

Left Lobby and stairs of theatre

Below Interior perspectives

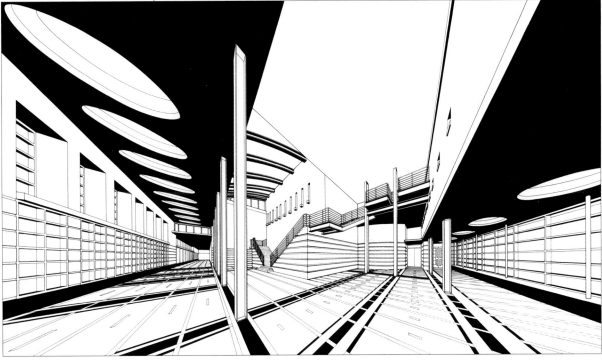

Right Detail of classrooms on courtyard with tower in distance

Below Repeatable and symbolic forms diagrams

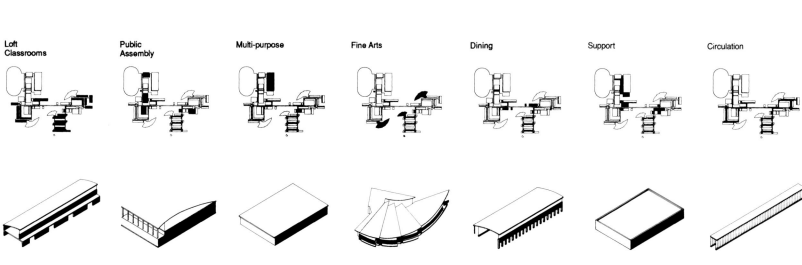

| Loft Classrooms | Public Assembly | Multi-purpose | Fine Arts | Dining | Support | Circulation |

Above Sports field with campus in background

Left High school gymnasium

Above Sports hall

Right Site plan

EVANGELISCHE GESAMTSCHULE GELSENKIRCHEN (EVANGELICAL SCHOOL IN GELSENKIRCHEN)

Gelsenkirchen-Bismarck, Germany

Peter Hübner and his office plus+ bauplanung won the IBA Emscher Park competition for this new evangelical school at Gelsenkirchen-Bismarck with an ecological theme that emphasised the natural progression of growth and change over time. It was a radical idea that entailed different building types and a team of architects and landscape architects, and the involvement of the local community.

From the nineteenth century, the town itself was host to a mining community. More recently, Gelsenkirchen has taken in many Turkish immigrant workers but has remained a grim industrial place. Poverty, unemployment and illiteracy were rampant, and the Protestant Church sought to ease these problems with a new school. Despite being a Protestant school, the student population consists of 30 per cent Muslim children and 25 per cent Catholics. Beyond educational aims, the school forms part of the wider community.

The new school is being built alongside an existing school building dating from the 1960s. Conceived as a village, the different types of new buildings cluster around a covered central spine with a piazza at the end, which also serves as the entrance. The entrance is marked by the cafeteria and library on either side, with music rooms and a chapel above. These are followed by the theatre, the administration rooms, and then the chemist and cinema, workshop and laboratory. The latter are teaching spaces but represent shops along a street. The complex ends in a court used by both students and the local community, and to the east of this is a large new sports hall.

Classroom blocks are being added as a series of side wings away from the central spine. At present four groups of five classrooms have been built, and another two are planned. The pupils were directly involved in the process of design and construction of the classrooms: architects worked up proposals based on the children's ideas, from which the children then built models. The architects then adjusted the designs in accordance with building regulations, before contractors erected the basic structures. Finishings were by pupils, teachers and parents. Encouraging children to participate in the design process has been an ideal of the school's director, who is a supporter of the Montessori and Dewey method of teaching.

Hübner's architectural signature comprises insulated concrete foundations topped by a lightweight construction in a timber frame. Roofs are either flat or gently angular, protected by membrane and covered in soil for growing plants. Thick insulation and glazing is designed for thermal efficiency, and so too are the classroom daylights. Smaller spaces use natural ventilation while the larger spaces (theatre and sports hall) use passive energy systems with a series of underground inlet pipes that are pre-warmed in winter and pre-cooled in summer (developed with Transsolar).

The children were also involved in the development of the gardens, and are required (by the landscape architect) to create gardens of vegetables, herbs or flowers as part of their education.

Entrance to library via a bridge across the pond

Evangelische Gesamtschule Gelsenkirchen

Top Classroom block at night

Centre Classroom block plan

Bottom Section

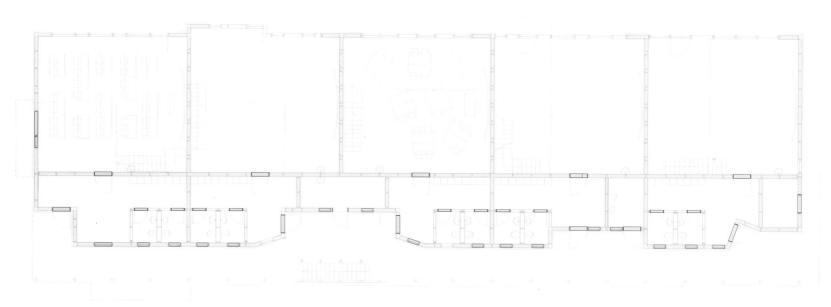

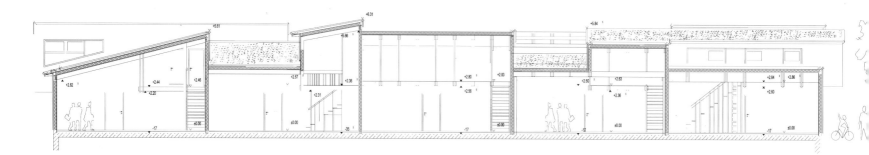

School Builders

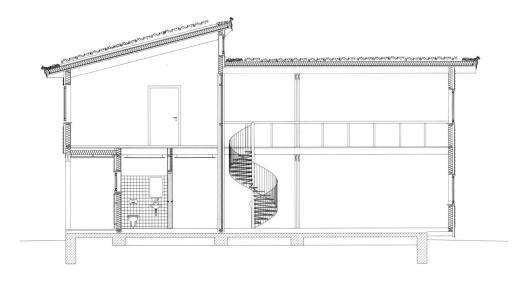

Top Section

Bottom Classroom block
with timber facade

Evangelische Gesamtschule Gelsenkirchen

Top Workshops in the round

Bottom Ground floor plan

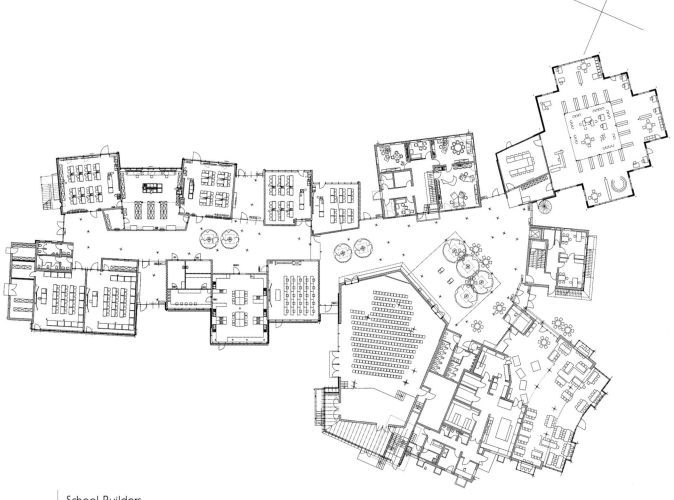

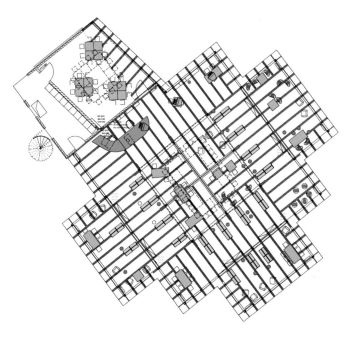

Top left Interior of hall

Top right Interior of cafeteria

Bottom left Interior of library

Bottom right Library plan

Top Part of central spine

Bottom The court of the central spine

School Builders

Upper level of central spine

WALDORF SCHOOL

Chorweiler, Cologne, Germany

The Waldorf School in Cologne had existed for seventeen years prior to Peter Hübner's design, but was housed in a former state school. Waldorf schooling follows the philosophy of Rudolf Steiner – 'anthroposophy'. There are many Steiner schools around Germany which aim to give children a much broader education than perhaps is attainable through state schools, and which focus on the importance of the development of social relations. Emphasis is placed especially on the arts and on the performing arts; thus Steiner schools typically have large auditoriums.

Hübner, known for his 'green' designs, was asked to produce a school with its own architectural identity that would reflect Steiner's philosophy.

The new school consists of two buildings organised around the two major social spaces – the sports hall and auditorium. Both are located to the north of the site: the sports hall is oriented to the northwest boundary and enjoys some winter solar gain; by contrast, the auditorium is sheltered by the main school. A 'street' runs through the two buildings, and this has to be used to reach the main entrance. An area of circular paving at the end of the street marks the beginning of the garden area.

The main school building comprises a radial three-storey arrangement facing from east through south to west. This arrangement opens inwards onto a central hall – the heart of the school – which also serves as the foyer to the auditorium. Its impressive glass roof, supported by tree-like columns, affords skylight and sunlight. This vertical hall also serves as the main ventilation shaft using the 'stack effect' to exhaust warm air through vents at the top, while sucking in fresh air at the bottom. Air is passed from a series of large, radially placed underground pipes: air can exchange heat with the mass of the earth under the building, being cooled in summer and warmed above zero in winter.

The classrooms were required to be neither boxlike nor rectangular, but more polygonal and open in character, and the needs of different types of activities were considered in the design and layout. Other rooms are more regular, but each has its own identity. Storage, ancillary and even the caretaker's apartment are tucked into the plan with great economy.

Even though it was a seemingly complex plan, by using concrete for the external walls and floors as well as timber roofs, the school managed to cost about 20 per cent below the average cost of a state school the same size. The staff, parents and children were continually involved in the design process which, according to the architects, helped the school take on a life of its own.

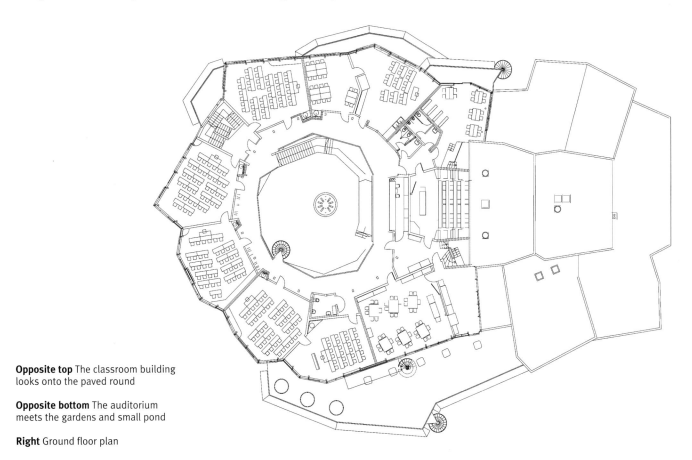

Opposite top The classroom building looks onto the paved round

Opposite bottom The auditorium meets the gardens and small pond

Right Ground floor plan

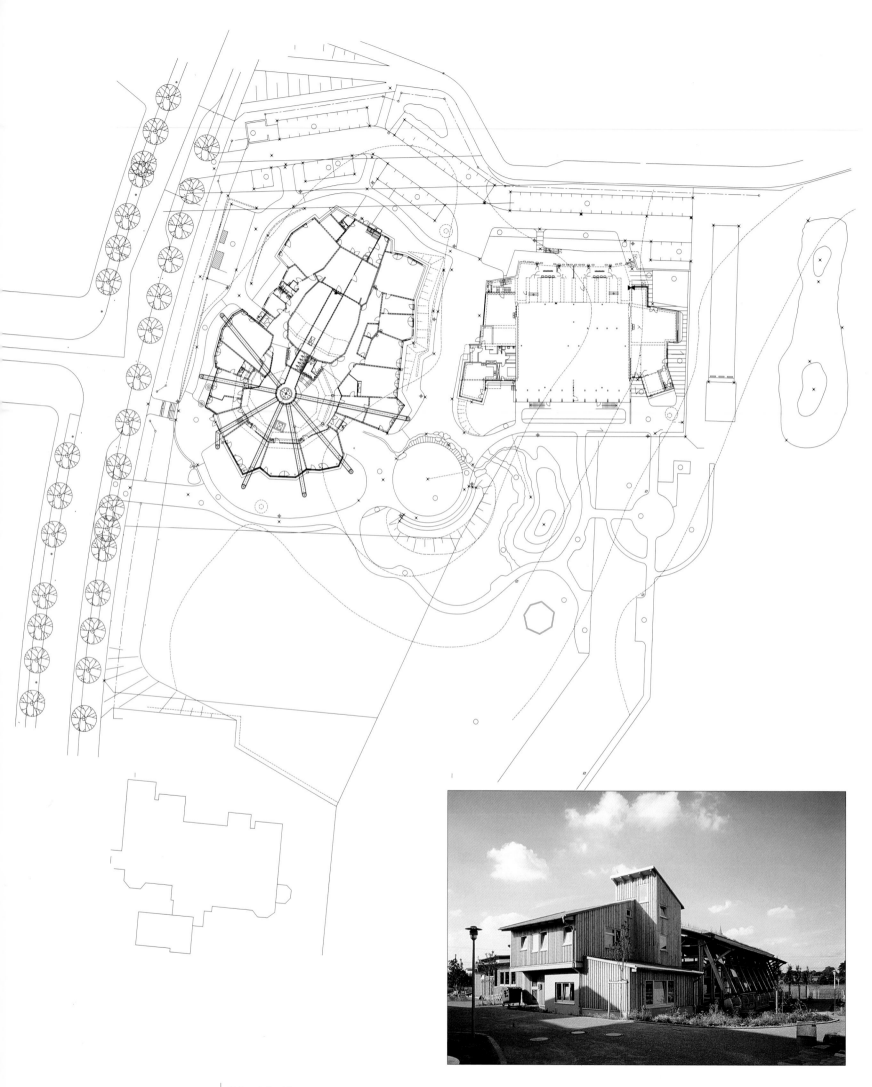

Opposite top Site plan

Opposite bottom View of sports hall

Above One of the classroom buildings

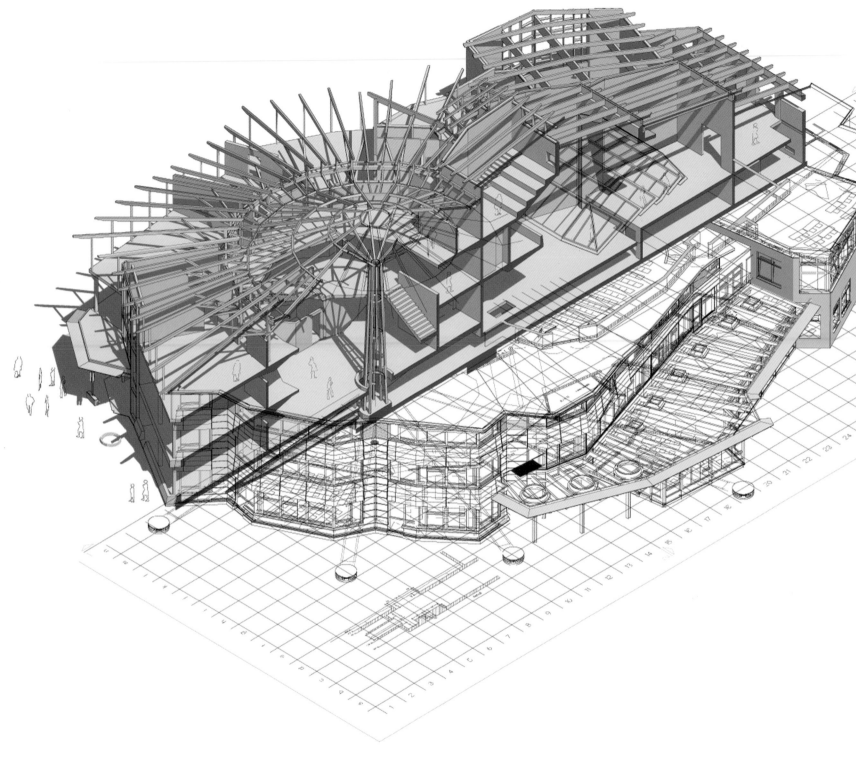

Above Section

Opposite top Section

Opposite bottom Stairs and walkways in main hall

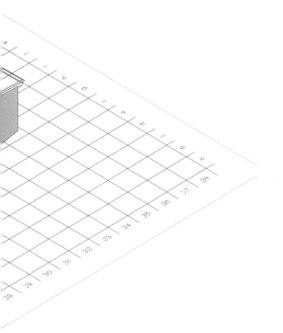

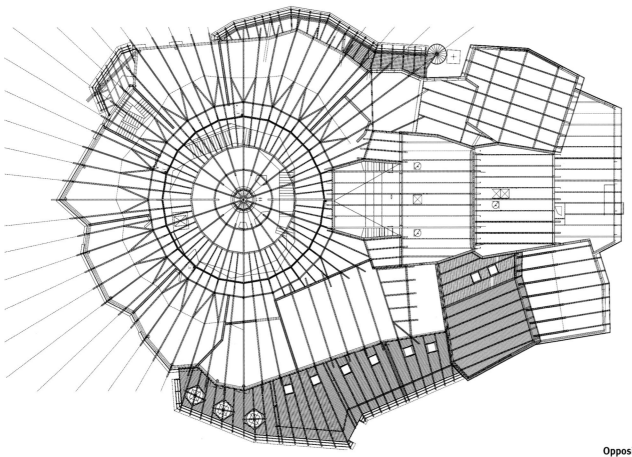

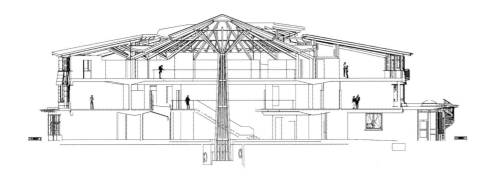

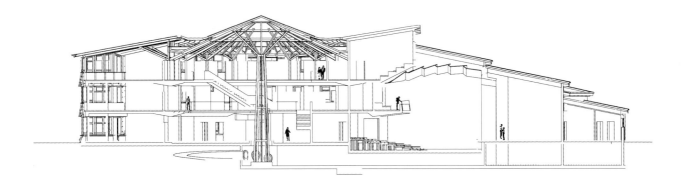

Opposite top The glass roof in the main hall is supported by treelike columns

Opposite bottom Main hall at ground level

Top Third floor plan

Centre and bottom Sections

Top Classrooms look out onto play area

Bottom First floor plan

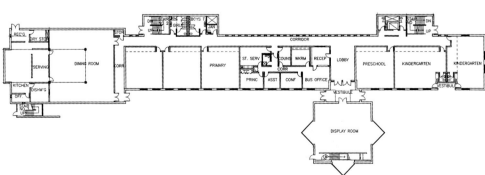

School Builders

CESAR CHAVEZ ELEMENTARY SCHOOL

Chicago, Illinois, US

The design of this public elementary school focuses on two issues: creating an identity for the new building and using the small urban site efficiently.

Sited on a fragment of a city block the school serves Chicago's gritty, gang-infested 'back-of-the-yards' Mexican-American neighbourhood, from kindergarten through to eighth grade. The three-storey single-loaded plan mitigates an unpleasant alley running alongside the site and maximises play space.

The site was restrictive, being only slightly larger than an acre, less than half the size of a standard school. To manage this, Ross Barney + Jankowski designed a long single-loaded classroom configuration with classrooms on just one side of the hallway (rather than the standard double-layout), and built a storey higher. This long, narrow design resulted in a much greater proportion of exterior wall than many school buildings yet at the same time achieved the same square footage.

The building consists of functional modules arranged on a single-loaded circulation spine, creating a walk to the alley while affording all the classrooms and playgrounds a view. The site opens to the community, allowing visual supervision from the surrounding houses and discouraging gang activities. There is a full-size gymnasium at one end of the classroom spine, unusually located on the second floor, although a staircase leads directly from the gymnasium to the playground. A display room and library are located in the cube volume near the front entrance to the school.

Five colours of brick on the exterior add colour to the otherwise grey urban context. Interiors utilise colours on the window frames and the floor tiles, adding an interesting detail to the interiors. Strong colour is carried into the interior corridors and common spaces, but the classrooms are finished in neutral white walls and natural wood to become a canvas for the creative and learning activity of the children. The pyramidal skylight in the library building provides natural illumination, and during the day the library itself is lit with skylights. The usual palette of concrete block and acoustic tile was expanded to include other inexpensive, durable materials. Chipboard is used as panelling in the lobby and corridors, and exposed concrete ceilings are painted sky-blue.

In addition, the architects included a basement to maximise square footage and minimise costs: this provided an additional 279 square metres (3,000 square feet) at a cost of just $50,000; the space is used for storage and housing mechanical equipment.

External elevation

Cesar Chavez Elementary School

Top Classroom looking out onto street

Bottom Second floor plan

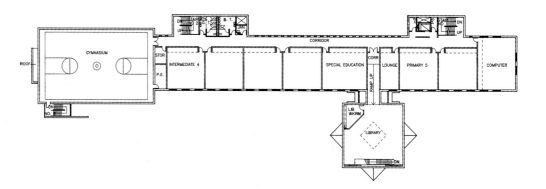

School Builders

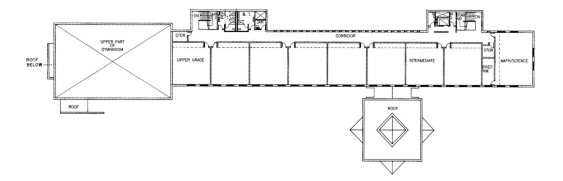

Top Third floor plan

Bottom Detail of corridor

Cesar Chavez Elementary School

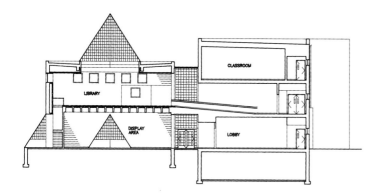

Opposite Detail of cafeteria

Top left Interior of library

Top right Interior doorway detail

Bottom Transverse section

School building from street

The Little Village Academy, a K-8 (kindergarten through to eight-year-olds) school, is located in the heart of Chicago's Mexican community. The site is of limited size, and therefore dictated a very efficient plant. It is bordered by commercial properties along Lawndale and 27th Street, and residential properties line the west and north.

To manage the small site, Ross Barney + Jankowski brought the school building right to the edge of the pavement on the east, leaving room for a large playground on the north side and a smaller play area for the kindergarten to the south.

The building is organised around a sun-themed central stair forming the functional and spiritual heart of the school while recalling the community's Mexican heritage. The curved, skylit stair enclosure is highlighted by a three-storey vertical sundial, which also marks the building's main entrance, and the grand stairwell is supported by three steel columns, which are less expensive than using cantilevers. The terrazzo sunburst floor originating at the sundial carries through the lobby and outdoor playground.

The architects designed the base building as a simple rectangular box with a compact floor plan, and used a load-bearing masonry structure (rather than steel frame) to save on costs. To enliven the exteriors at low cost, they combined a rough-faced brick with burnished brick, and used bold colours such as blue and yellow.

The third-floor library that rises above the flat roof is a porcelain-and-glass box suspended in the larger structure. Clerestory windows are on all sides, and the shafts of floor-to-ceiling glass at the two corners bring plenty of sunlight into the room. The science rooms have translucent fibreglass panels to let in sunlight without the glare.

Materials for the 6,320-square-metre (68,000-square-foot) $7 million project were selected for their cost-effectiveness and durability. Major finishes include split and ground face concrete block, glazed brick and block, and chipboard panelling.

Awards

American Institute of Architects (AIA) Institute Honor Award For Architecture (2000), Institute Honor Award for Interior Architecture (1999), Chicago Building Congress Merit Award (1998), Richard H Driehaus Foundation Award for Architectural Excellence in Community Design (1998), AIA Chicago Distinguished Building Award (1997), AIA Chicago Interior Architecture Award (1997), Illinois Association of School Boards Exhibition of School Architecture (1996).

View from inside school yard

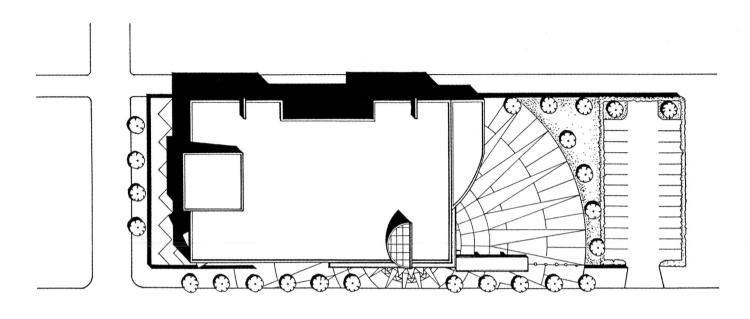

Top Site plan

Bottom Interior of cafeteria

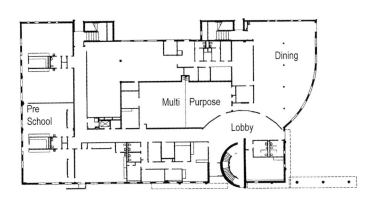

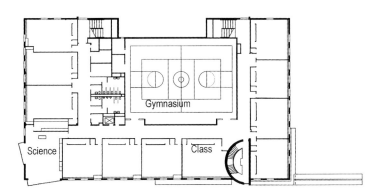

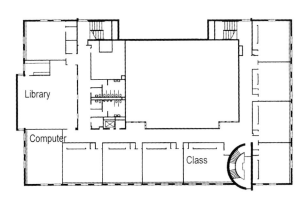

Left top First floor plan

Left centre Second floor plan

Left bottom Third floor plan

Right top External view of library

Right bottom Interior corridor

Little Village Academy

Left External view of three-storey sundial and stairwell

Right Looking down the staircase of the sundial

Opposite Internal view of sundial and stairwell

School Builders

Little Village Academy

Top View of school from street

Bottom Ground floor plan
1 Office
2 Storage
3 Conference room
4 Reception
5 Classroom
6 Faculty/Staff lounge
7 Student lounge
8 Restroom

Opposite left Side-street view of school

Opposite right View of school from street

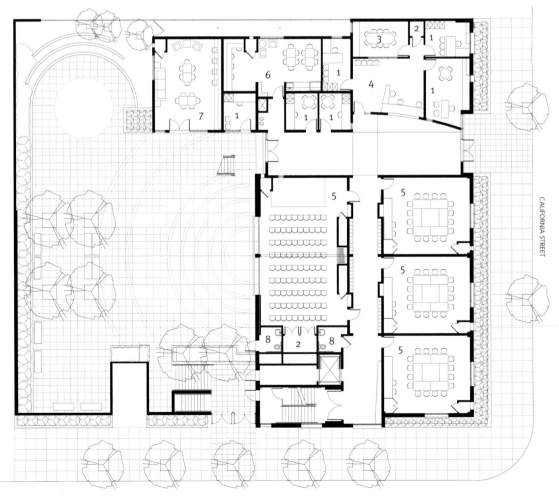

CALIFORNIA STREET

BRODERICK STREET

School Builders

DREW COLLEGE PREPARATORY SCHOOL

Drew College Preparatory School, a private high school in San Francisco, had occupied a Victorian house since 1908 and later motel-like extensions had been wedged onto the house. The deteriorating campus needed renovation to keep up with the curriculum, and its lack of proper teaching structures had a negative affect on the intake to the school. The school therefore sought funds to build a new school on the original urban site.

The new contemporary school building designed by SMWM is a 3,250-square-metre (35,000-square-foot) three-storey L-shaped structure stacked on top of a 1,390-square-metre (15,000-square-foot) concrete parking podium with a courtyard in its L. Design is efficient to make the best use of the small space available: the classrooms are small with flexible seating that can be rearranged for group learning or individual study. The building has state-of-the-art science labs, art rooms, support spaces and a lecture hall, features topped by a double-height, light-filled corner library. An opening to the courtyard placed two-thirds of the way into the long leg of the L, shortens circulation pathways.

The design was also influenced by the local urban characteristics of neighbouring Victorian family houses and the various styles of family buildings through the use of brick in the facade. In addition, SMWM introduced contemporary materials such as glass, steel and concrete, and lifted the roof at the corner so that it climbs high above the street and gives the building a strong presence.

According to the school head 'This building was an instant source of pride. It has changed our perceptions of ourselves and prompted higher-quality teaching and higher self-expectations from our students' (*Architectural Record's Building Type Studies*, February 2002).

LICK-WILMERDING HIGH SCHOOL

San Francisco, California, US

Lick-Wilmerding High School, founded in 1895 in San Francisco, has always maintained a strong commitment to arts programmes. However, its curriculum outgrew its campus and SMWM Architects were asked to design a new masterplan for the school, including a new library.

Their solution transformed a collection of connected buildings into a campus, using the large field as the central green, surrounded by buildings on three sides. The fourth side of the field is open-ended, facing views of the city beyond, a metaphor for the school's internal organisation and its relationship to the community.

The new library was placed on the south side of the campus between a neighbourhood of single-family houses facing south and the quadrangle of the campus to its north. A flat-roofed classroom wing facing the street shields a vaulted structure on the campus side; separation between the two is marked by a brightly coloured 12-metre-high (38-foot-high) wall running the length of the building. The library building is a wood frame with plywood shear walls, with glulam-and-steel-rod roof trusses exposed in the main reading room.

The east–west corridor on the ground floor was designed with lit alcoves to function as a long gallery for the exhibition of students' work.

The architects used flat and corrugated cement panels in a grid to provide an interesting play of light throughout the campus. The panels themselves make reference to the industrial character of the existing buildings. The interiors are derived from the exteriors: the library exposes the structural elements of the library's vaulted roof and cement-panel fasteners, and the Italian plaster finish and stained concrete afford better wear and tear. In addition, to entice students to spend time in the library, the school looked at retailing concepts deployed at popular stores such as Barnes & Noble, thus the library is fully equipped with scanners, CD-writers, a sound-dubbing system, a copy centre and a lounge leading on to a balcony giving views of the city.

Opposite top External view of school from street

Opposite bottom External view of side of school

Above left Internal view of library

Above right Internal view of art room

Above External view across park

Left Site plan

Right Sketch

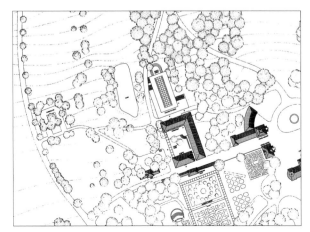

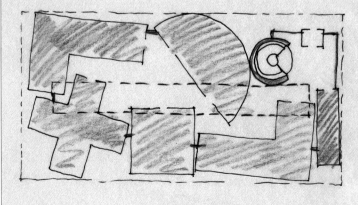

School Builders

Thomas van den Valentyn architektur & S Mohammed Oreyzi

MUSIKGYMNASIUMS SCHLOß BELVEDERE BEI WEIMAR
(MUSIC HIGH SCHOOL IN WEIMAR)

Weimar, Germany

The Music High School in Weimar, is situated in the heart of Bauhaus country, it is the only music school for musically gifted boys and girls in Germany. It accommodates 130 students who board. Architect Valentyn and his collaborator Oreyzi won the competition to design the school, the DM20 million donation for which came from Deutsche Bank AG in order to mark the bank's 125th anniversary.

The original buildings defined the plan of the site with a U-shaped court-yard, and as they were listed, had to be incorporated into the new plan. Conservation orders also dictated that the old buildings should be reno-vated with authentic construction: thick walls without the use of metal support, and wooden windows without silicon. The old inn (c 1730–40) was completely renovated due to damp in 1995/96, and now houses some of the boarding and practising rooms and the administration for both. The old barn was mostly rebuilt, based on the original form with the same pro-portions, and now houses 65 two-person boarding rooms and the canteen with a terrace.

The new building is designed in a classic modern style using a strictly minimalist language, paying homage to the white modern architecture of the 1919 Bauhaus. The new interiors are functional and comfortable. The carpets are a rich pastel blue; wood is used for the floors and wall-panelling, and the walls and ceilings are of white plaster.

The school is entered where the mezzanine is on ground level. It is a bright yard made of glass, with a patio, and the five geometrically mod-elled rooms are placed like houses on alleys and squares. The facades are made of a shipbuilders' plywood stained in orange – a sort of 'violin-esque lustre'. The patio allows extended views across the park and up through the wide-cut open upper-storey where eight classrooms and a library are arranged along a gallery. A straight steel staircase, constructed intention-ally at a slightly slanting angle, leads from the mezzanine to the upper floor. Most of the daylight enters through the glass roof. At the entrance a spacious spiral staircase in a reflecting glass cylinder winds down to the lower level of a large auditorium where four steps of tiered seating accom-modate an audience of up to 400.

Square concrete pillars – the lower-half wood-panelled and the upper made of concrete – form an 'austere' and 'solemn' (sic) far-stretched 'U' inside the rectangular space. Inside, a sophisticated lighting system is embedded in the dark-blue ceiling. The acoustic quality of the space is of a very high standard – with a reverberation up to 2.4 to 1.6 seconds.

Looking through the glass front of the auditorium

Musikgymnasiums Schloß Belvedere bei Weimar

Top External elevation

Bottom Ground floor plan

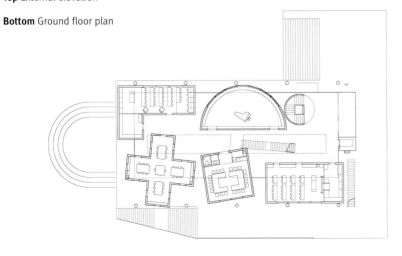

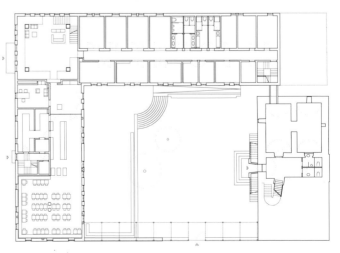

School Builders

Top Auditorium

Bottom Plan of large music hall

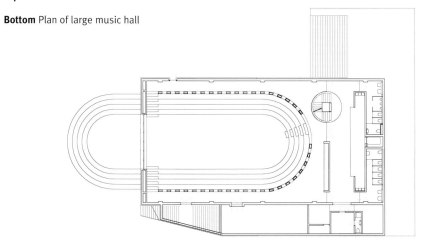

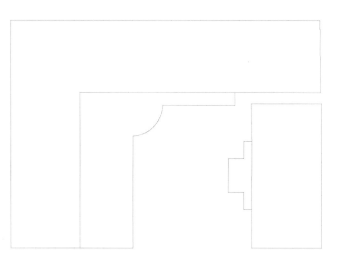

Musikgymnasiums Schloß Belvedere bei Weimar

Top Detail of classroom with colourful chairs

Bottom Elevation

Opposite top Music room with panoramic window

Opposite bottom Detail of auditorium

School Builders

Musikgymnasiums Schloß Belvedere bei Weimar

Internal stairs leading to mezzanine and down to auditorium

Musikgymnasiums Schloß Belvedere bei Weimar

Above Front of school with children in play areas

Below Sections

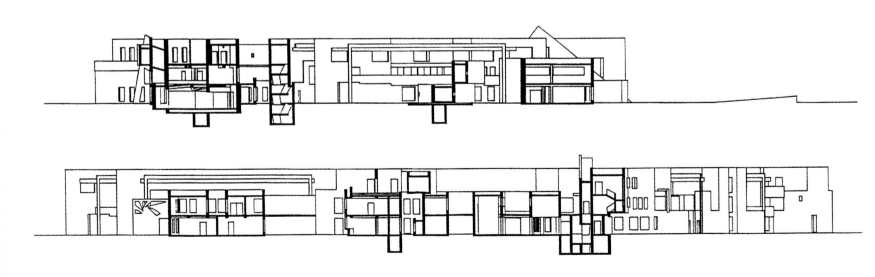

Zvi Hecker

JEWISH PRIMARY SCHOOL BERLIN

Berlin, Germany

An organic, unfolding space, the Jewish Primary School in Berlin is especially symbolic, being the first of its kind since the Second World War.

The school has been designed like a little village, with walkways, dead-end streets and passageways. It is also playful in its design, with many corners and curves, and labyrinth-like corridors within which to play and hide. The school comprises typical large functional spaces and small classrooms. The large hall doubles up as a synagogue with a capacity for 500, and the dining hall has two kitchens (meat and milk) in respect of Jewish culinary traditions.

Safety is high on the agenda within this closed, inward-looking school, but at the same time the plan follows a unique, organic and playful shape.

The architect says: 'The school was designed in the form of a flower, as a gift to the children of Berlin. The sunflower's celestial construction seemed most suitable for planning the school, since its seeds orbit the sun and the sun's rays illuminate all of the schoolrooms.

'Berlin accepted the gift and entrusted us with the work. To begin with, calculations had to be made of the sun's orbits and the length of all its rays. When these were completed, construction could begin. Bricks were brought and laid one over the other. Walls rose and the building began to emerge.

'In time it became evident that the school, whilst under construction, was gradually transforming into an intricate city. Streets and paths followed the orbits and the infinitesimal traces of the sun's rays. The exterior moulded the city's interior into a mirror of the universe, a place where light and shadow intersect. Children loved it and the work continued.'

Back view of school

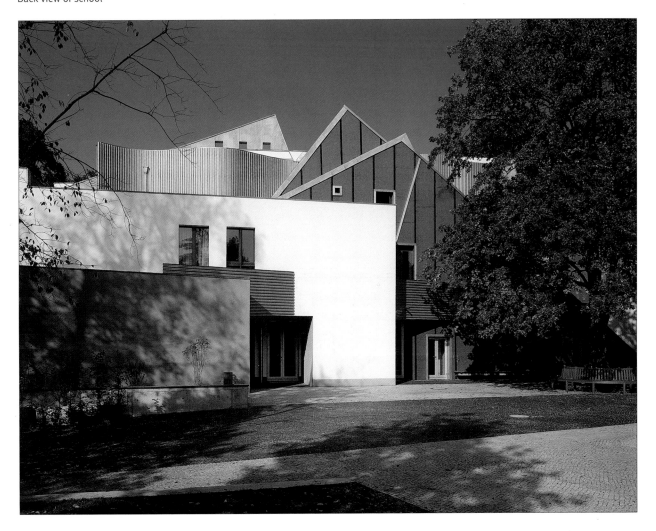

Opposite top Interior from roof

Opposite bottom Interior showing curved walls and interlocking spaces

Above Aerial view of school showing 'flower' form

Right Sketch

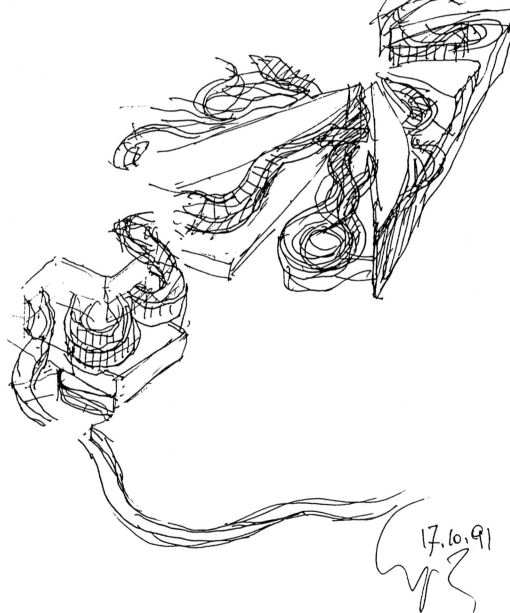

17.10.91

Jewish Primary School Berlin

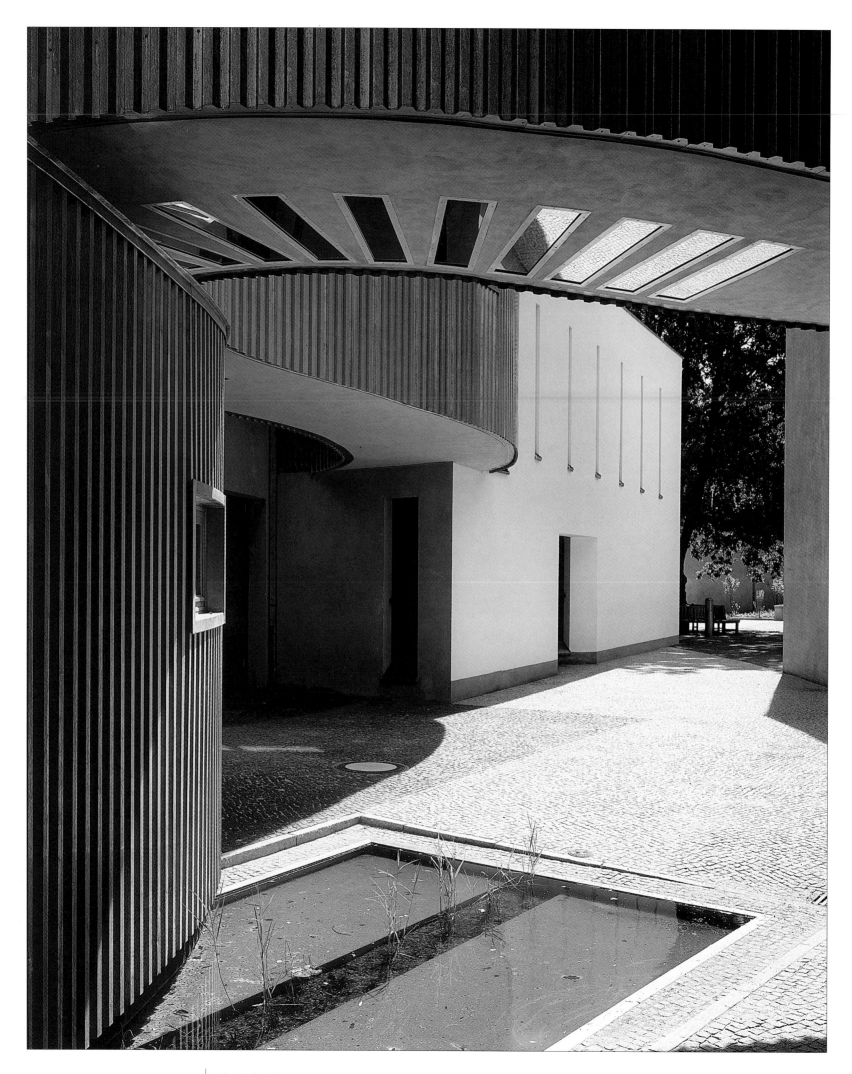

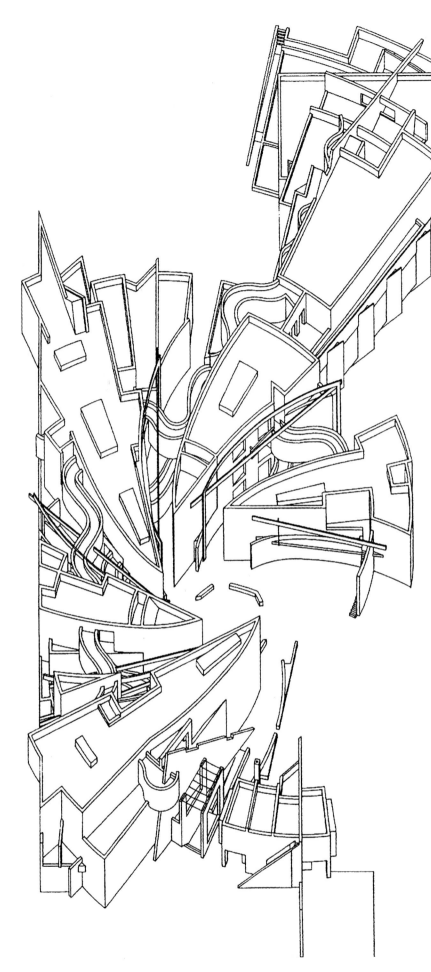

Opposite Small pond of water under curving walkway

Left Axonometric section

Right Curved walls and corridors inside school area

Jewish Primary School Berlin

Left Ground floor plan

Right Corridor interior

Above Large hall also used as synagogue

Left Sketch

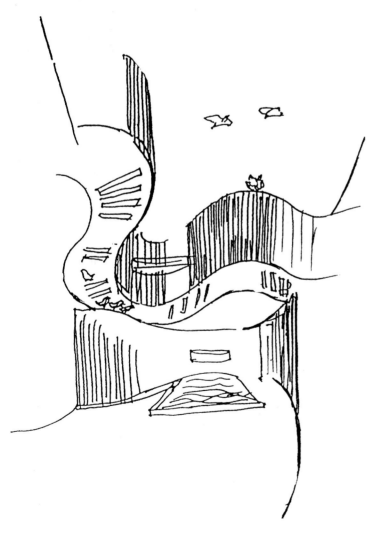

PROJECT INFORMATION

The following information has been collated from material provided by the architects. All costs should be taken as a guide only.

ALLFORD HALL MONAGHAN MORRIS
Great Notley Primary School, Essex, England
Commissioned by: Essex County Council
Structural engineer: Atelier One
Environmental engineer: Atelier Ten
Landscape architect: Jonathan Watkins Landscape
Quantity surveyor: Cook & Butler
Public artist: Kovats and Hartley
Planning supervisor: Appleyard & Trew
Cost: £1.25 million
Total area of site: 1,044m^2 (11,238ft^2)
Design to completion: 41 weeks, 1998–99
Number of students: 180 but will eventually take 300
Number of classrooms: 6
Materials: Cedar external cladding, Sedum roof covering, Plyboo bamboo flooring, timber 'breathing wall' Warmcel insulation, masonite beams

ARBEIDSGRUPPEN HUS
Steinerskolen I Stavanger, Stavanger, Norway
Speciality: Steiner school
Project team: Led by Espen Tharalsden. Team: Sverre Øystein Woxen, Ole Rasmus Nygaard, Svein Erik Tøien
Commissioned by: Stiftelsen Steinerskolen
Cost: Nok29 million
Total area of site: 12,000m^2 (129,168ft^2)
Completed: In phases 1991, 1995, 1999, and ongoing
Number of students: 320
Number of classrooms: 12

ARCHITECTURE PLB
Haute Vallée School, Jersey, Channel Islands, England
Speciality: Secondary school
Designed by: Richard Jobson
Project team: Ian Deans, Rod Graham, Andrew Nichol, Billy Prendergast, Mike Skilton, John Waldron
Commissioned by: States of Jersey Education Committee
Cost: £14.06 million
Total area of site: 9,300m^2 (100,105ft^2)
Completed: 2002
Number of students: 750
Number of classrooms: 24

ARUP ASSOCIATES (LONDON)
Druk White Lotus School, Ladakh, India
Speciality: Charitable school using low-tech solutions
Project team: Led by Johnathon Rose, James Fleming.
Commissioned by: Drukpa Trust
Cost: £2 million
Design to completion: Phased from 1998–2010
Number of students: 80–800
Materials: Local stone, mud brick.
Special features: Tibetan temple

BEHNISCH & PARTNER
Montessori School Ingolstadt, Hollerstauden, Germany
Speciality: Kindergarten, primary and secondary school
Project architect: Beckus Beckmann
Project team: Matias Stumpfl, Jochen Schmid, Andreas Ditschuneit, Anke Bosch, Liv Johannson, Jörg Meiers, Oliver Sippl, Stefanie Wirth, Günter Zuckriegel
Colours: Christian Kandzia

Site architects: Hagen Ruff, Peter Albrecht, Oliver Degen
Commissioned by: Society for Integrated Education in Kindergartens and Schools, Ingolstadt
Cost: DM14.5 million
Number of students: 330
Number of classrooms: 24 (plus kindergarten)
Design to completion: 1993–96

BEHNISCH & PARTNER
Vocational School, Öhringen, Germany
Project architect: Dagmar Schork
Project team: Sandra Seibold, Jürgen Mattman, Martina Höh
Site architects: Sigrid Duffner, Armin Gebert, Wolfgang Leukel
Commissioned by: Hohenlohekreis (district office)
Cost: DM35.5 million
Total area of site: 6,446m^2 (69,385 square feet)
Completed: 1993
Number of students: 650
Number of classrooms: 27

BUILDING DESIGN PARTNERSHIP
Hampden Gurney School, London, England
Speciality: Church of England primary school
Structural engineer, building services engineer, quantity surveyor, lighting design: Building Design Partnership
Project team: Charles Broughton, Dominic Church, Susanna Dobson, Paul Gibbins, Gareth Jones, Tony McGuirk (architect director), Ann Marsh, Helen Maudslay, Keith Papa, Ray Springer, John Toovey
Commissioned by: Head of the Trustees, Father Michael Burgess and the Trustees of Hampden Gurney School
Cost: £6 million
Total area of site: 3,615.7m^2 (38,919ft^2)
Design to completion: 2000–02
Number of students: 210 primary, 30 nursery
Number of classrooms: 6
Materials: Concrete, steel, tensile structures, glass
Special features: Chapel, six external play areas – lower ground, ground, first, second, third, fourth floors

DOUGHERTY & DOUGHERTY ARCHITECTS LLP
Rio del Norte Elementary School, Oxnard, California, US
Speciality: Extended daycare on site and joint use of playing fields
Project team: Brian P Dougherty (partner-in-charge), Brian Dougherty and Neill Noble (designers), Cymbre Potter (job captain)
Commissioned by: Rio School District
Cost: $7.3 million
Total area of site: 4-hectare (10-acre) site, 4,180m^2 (45,000ft^2) of school
Design to completion: 1997–2001
Number of students: 650
Number of classrooms: 26
Materials: Concrete, exterior plaster, exposed steel

ELDER AND CANNON ARCHITECTS
St Aloysius Junior School, Garnethill, Glasgow, Scotland
Speciality: Jesuit school
Commissioned by: Trustees of St Aloysius College
Cost: £2.3 million

Total area of site: 784m^2 (8,439ft^2), 2,500m^2 (26,910ft^2) floor area over five floors
Design to completion: 24 months
Number of students: 450
Number of classrooms: 18
Special features: Computer-controlled motorised glass louvres which take into account exact location of the sun

HAMPSHIRE COUNTY COUNCIL ARCHITECTS
Queens Inclosure First School, Hampshire, England
Special details: Greenfield site adjacent to woods
Project team: Led by Dave Morris and Alec Upton
Commissioned by: Hampshire County Council Education Department
Cost: £1.3 million
Total area of site: 4 hectares (10 acres)
Design to completion: 1986–88 (phase two 1996–7)
Number of students: 420
Number of classrooms: 14
Materials: Steel, aluminium, glass

HAMPSHIRE COUNTY COUNCIL ARCHITECTS
Stakes Hill Infant School, Hampshire, England
Special details: Set in former park, adjacent to woods, sharing site with existing junior school
Project team: Led by Mike Keys
Commissioned by: Hampshire County Council Education Department
Cost: £1.35 million
Total area of site: 4 hectares (10 acres)
Design to completion: 1994–96
Number of students: 270
Number of classrooms: 10
Materials: Mostly timber

HAMPSHIRE COUNTY COUNCIL ARCHITECTS
Whiteley Primary School, Hampshire, England
Special details: Set in remnants of woodland, adjacent to dense wood, extension of original building
Project team: Led by Nev Churcher and David Woolfenden
Commissioned by: Hampshire County Council Education Department
Cost: £3 million
Total area of site: 3.2 hectares (8 acres), including woods
Design to completion: 1997–2000 (two phases)
Number of pupils: 630
Number of classrooms: 21

HAMPSHIRE COUNTY COUNCIL ARCHITECTS
Woodlea Primary School, Hampshire, England
Special details: Situated in dense woodland on steep slope, below an Iron Age fort
Project team: Led by Nev Churcher and Sally Daniels
Commissioned by: Hampshire County Council Education Department
Cost: £1.2 million
Total area of site: 2.4 hectares (6 acres) of mixed woodland
Design to completion: 1989–91
Number of students: 210
Number of classrooms: 7
Materials: Mostly timber

HEIN GOLDSTEIN ARCHITECT
Oskar-Maria-Graf-Gymnasium (Oskar-Maria-Graf Secondary School), Neufahrn, Germany
Speciality: Secondary school
Project team: Hein Goldstein, Thomas Baerwolf, Bernd Greger, Stefan Hassenzahl, Thomas Kubsa, Richard Bessing, Laura Fischer, Inge Lutz, Martina Stoiber
Commissioned by: Zweckverband Staatliches Gymnasium Neufahrn bei Freising
Cost: DM42 million
Total area of site: 10,000m² (107,640ft²)
Design to completion: 2.5 years
Number of students: 900
Number of classrooms: 28 plus speciality classrooms and senior common rooms
Materials: Highly efficient heat insulating glazing, Kerto timber cladding, anodised Alucobond, facing concrete, horizontal glazing, terrazzo, linoleum, parquetry, rubber

ITSUKO HASEGAWA
Kaiho Elementary School, Himi, Japan
Design to completion: 1993–96
(Further information unavailable)

KUMPULAN AKITEK
Lycée Français de Singapour (International French School of Singapore)
Speciality: Three–in-one school including kindergarten, primary and secondary
Commissioned by: Lycée Française de Singapour Ltd
Cost: $11 million
Total area of site: 25,000m² (269,100ft²), built area 16,000m² (172,224ft²)
Design to completion: 1997–99
Number of students: 1,000
Number of classrooms: 40
Materials: Timber-clad wall (kindergarten), fair-faced brick (primary), steel and glass (secondary)

LORD, AECK & SARGENT
Trinity School, Atlanta, Georgia, US
Special details: Renovation and expansion to existing private elementary school
Project team: Terry Sargent, Betsy Beaman, Allen Duncan, Michael Few, Jimmy Hawkins, Harriet Leavens, Larry Lord, Howard Wertheimer.
Commissioned by: Trinity School
Cost: $3 million
Total construction area: 2,183m² (23,500ft²), campus in total 3.2 hectares (8 acres)
Design to completion: over period 1986–98
Number of students: 500

PATKAU ARCHITECTS
Strawberry Vale Elementary School, British Columbia, Canada
Project team: Grace Cheung, Michael Cunningham, Michael Kothke, Tim Newton, John Patkau, Patricia Patkau, Peter Suter, Allan Teramura, John Wall, Jacqueline Wang
Commissioned by: The Greater Victoria School District
Cost: CAN $10 million
Total area of site: 3,292m² (35,435ft²)
Number of students: 450
Number of classrooms: 16
Materials: Mostly wood

PERKINS & WILL IN ASSOCIATION WITH MIMBRES INC
Desert View Elementary School, New Mexico, US
Special details: Single-storey elementary school, winner of AIA National Honour Award
Project team: Ralph Johnson (design principal), John Arzarian (project designer), James Toya (project manager), Kas Gemanas (project architect), Sam Jamron (project architect), Jerry Johnson, Elizabeth Fakatselis, Pamela Kurz, Mark Romack, Stuart Royalty, Carloyn Smith
Commissioned by: Gadsden Independent School District
Cost: $9.3 million for three schools
Total area of site: 10 hectares (25 acres)

Design to completion: 1986–87
Number of students: 600 students

PERKINS & WILL IN ASSOCIATION WITH PARKER/MUDGETT/SMITH ARCHITECTS
North Fort Myers School, North Fort Myers, Florida, US
Special details: AIA Honour Award 1995
Project team: Ralph E Johnson (design principal), C W Brubaker (managing principal), Jerry Johnson (project designer), James Woods (project manager), Brian Junge (illustrations), Celeste Robbins, Steve Roberts, Thomas Vecchio
Commissioned by: Lee County School Board
Cost: $14.1 million
Total area of site: 13 hectares (32 acres)
Design to completion: 1992–95
Number of students: 1,600

PERKINS & WILL IN ASSOCIATION WITH BURGESS & NIPLE
Perry Community Education Village, Perry, Ohio, US
Special details: K12 campus includes K-4 school, 5–8 school, high school and community fitness centre
Project team: Ralph Johnson (planning principal), Raymond Bordwell (project director), James Toya (project manager), August Battaglia (project designer), James Woods (project designer), William Schmalz (technical coordinator), James Nowak (technical coordinator), Eric Spielman, Michael Palmer, Jerry Johnson, Gregory Bennett, Carlos Parilla, Robin Randall, Celeste Robbins, Robert Ruggles, Randy Takahashi
Commissioned by: Perry Local School District
Cost: $95 million
Total area of site: 65 hectares (160 acres)
Design to completion: 1988–95 (all phases)
Number of students: 4,500

PLUS+ BAUPLANUNG
Evangelische Gesamtschule Gelsenkirchen (Evangelical School in Gelsenkirchen), Gelsenkirchen-Bismarck, Germany
Project team: Peter Hübner, Martin Busch, Klaus Eggler, Ulrike Engelhardt, Christoph Forster, Matthias Gulde, Bärbel Hübner, Olaf Hübner, Anja Keinath, Udo Keitel, Martin Müller, Stefan Nix-Pauleit, Patrick Remy, Akiko Shirota, Thomas Strähle, Harald Strupp
Engineers: Weischede und Partner
Energy concept: Transsolar
Commissioned by: Evangelische Schule in Westfalen eV
Cost: DM23 million
Total area of site: 46,000m² (495,145ft²)
Design to completion: 1997–2005
Number of students: 1,300 at final stage
Number of classrooms: 39
Materials: Grass roof, natural wood facade
Special features: Theatre, chapel, atrium

PLUS+ BAUPLANUNG
Waldorf School, Chorweiler, Cologne, Germany
Speciality: Steiner school
Project team: Peter Hübner, Klaus Eggler, Stefan Nix-Pauleit, Matthias Gulde, Paula Harkness, Angela Wellershaus
Structural engineer: Sobek & Reiger
Energy concept: Transsolar
Commissioned by: Waldorfpädagogik eV
Cost: DM10 million
Total area of site: 20,000m² (215,28oft²)
Design to completion: 1993–95
Number of students: 450
Number of classrooms: 20
Materials: Grass roof, glass roof in atrium
Special features: Auditorium, atrium

ROSS BARNEY + JANKOWSKI INC
Cesar Chavez Multicultural Academic Center, Chicago, Illinois, US
Special details: Very tight urban site
Project team: Carol Ross Barney (design principal), Alan Kirkpatrick (project architect)

Commissioned by: Ms Sandy Trabak, School Principal
Cost: $5.2 million
Total area of site: 5,945m² (64,000ft²)
Completed: 1993
Number of students: designed for 550, now holds 750

ROSS BARNEY + JANKOWSKI INC
Little Village Academy, Chicago, Illinois, US
Special details: Small site
Project team: Carol Ross Barney (design principal), Alan Kirkpatrick (project architect), Deborah Burkhart (project manager), Sallie Schwartzkopf, Eric Martin
Commissioned by: Little Village Academy
Cost: $7 million
Total area of site: 6,320m² (68,000ft²)
Completed: 1996

SMWM ARCHITECTS
Drew College Preparatory School, San Francisco, California, US
Project team: Cathy Simon (principal in charge), Liza Pannozzo (project architect), John Long (project manager), Barbara Shands (designer), Diane Lam (interior designer), Tim Potter (job captain), James Koentopp (construction contract administrator)
Commissioned by: Drew College Preparatory School
Cost: $7.75 million
Total area of site: 3,250m² (35,000ft²)
Design to completion: 1997–2001
Number of students: 210
Number of classrooms: 8
Materials: Brick, glass, steel, concrete
Special features: Library/learning resource area

SMWM ARCHITECTS
Lick-Wilmerding High School, San Francisco, California, US
Special details: 745m² of 1,580m² (8,000ft² of 17,000ft²) is dedicated to the second-floor library
Project team: Cathy Simon (principal in charge), John Long (project manager), Liza Pannozzo (project architect), Alyosha Verzhbinsky (masterplan), Donald Cremers (interiors), Stephen Phillips, Dan Ceetham
Commissioned by: Lick-Wilmerding High School
Cost: $2.95 million
Total area of site: 1,580m² (17,000ft²)
Design to completion: 1991–97
Number of students: 381
Materials: Flat and corrugated cement board, operable aluminium windows, metal roof and hand-trowelled integral colour plaster

THOMAS VAN DEN VALENTYN ARCHITEKTUR & S MOHAMMED OREYZI
Musikgymnasiums Schloß Belvedere bei Weimar (Music High School in Weimar), Weimar, Germany
Speciality: Private school for young talented musicians
Project team: Thomas van den Valentyn, S Mohammed Oreyzi, Harms and Partner, Otto Reinbeck
Commissioned/funded by: Deutsche Bank AG (competition)
Cost: DM20 million
Design to completion: 1995–96
Number of students: 130 (boarding)
Special features: Dormitories

ZVI HECKER
Jewish Primary School Berlin, Berlin, Germany
Special details: First Jewish primary school in Berlin since Second World War
Project team: Zvi Hecker with Peter Kever, David Evans
Commissioned by: Jewish Primary School of Berlin
Cost: DM32 million
Total area of site: 16,400m² (176,530ft²)
Design to completion: 1991–95
Number of students: 800
Materials: Concrete, brick, corrugated metal cladding
Special features: Communal assembly hall for 500 doubles as a synagogue